No Ordinary Wedding Planner

Naomi was 26 when she was diagnosed with breast cancer, only two days after her boyfriend had proposed. After fulfilling her dream of getting married thanks to the generosity of local companies, she decided to set up The Wedding Wishing Well Foundation. Through her charity, currently based in South-West England, she now organises and funds weddings for those who are terminally ill.

No Ordinary Wedding Planner

Fighting against the odds
to help others make
their dreams come true

Naomi Thomas

Harper
TrueLife

HarperTrueLife
An imprint of HarperCollins*Publishers*
77–85 Fulham Palace Road,
Hammersmith, London W6 8JB

www.harpertrue.com
www.harpercollins.co.uk

First published by HarperTrueLife 2014

1 3 5 7 9 10 8 6 4 2

© Naomi Thomas 2014

Naomi Thomas asserts the moral right to
be identified as the author of this work

A catalogue record of this book is
available from the British Library

PB ISBN: 978-0-00-810507-5
EB ISBN: 978-0-00-758394-2

Chapter One

New Year's Eve 2009 was fast approaching. I was 26, and I worked and partied – hard! My first marriage had come to an end, and although my husband and I had separated amicably, I had been with him since the age of 16 and it had been a shock to the system to be on my own. You could say I was making up for lost time! Workwise, I loved my job. I was employed by Exeter City Council to run holiday play schemes for children from deprived areas of the city; it was one of the most rewarding jobs I had ever had, and I loved the kids and my colleagues. I was also working part time running my own business as a wedding planner, as well as assisting local venues as their in-house planner. Holding down two jobs was tiring, but I loved every moment – I felt as if life couldn't have been any better, and I wanted to celebrate.

I discovered that my favourite DJ was playing at my local haunt and immediately made plans to see in the New Year with my friends and beloved music.

The evening was an absolute blast! As with every New Year, I decided it was about time I changed a few things – I wanted to leave the past behind me, and to be happy in my own company. I had become a real gym junkie in 2008 and was hoping to continue the hard work by completing some charity fun runs and training for the London Marathon. I had lost over a stone and was starting to feel much more confident about myself. As 2010 began, I finally felt in control of my life. Little did I know that it wouldn't last long!

My New Year's resolutions started off well, although they began to dwindle as January came to an end. I was still feeling a little dented from the end of my marriage and discovered that a very old friend of mine seemed to be going through something similar. Graham and I had known each other since we were about 14 or 15, when he worked in the local pub that I used to frequent, back when I looked much older than I was. He had a real presence when he arrived at the bar on a Saturday night; everyone would be shaking his hand and patting him on the back when he walked in, fashionably late! Although I can't say I fancied him then there was certainly something about him, and when we became friends on Facebook I noticed that he had definitely improved with age! As Graham had a girlfriend, I had never thought any more of it, but now that his Facebook status suggested it was over I decided to take the plunge and message him.

Graham responded almost immediately, confirming that they had indeed broken up that week. This was my chance! Three days of flirty text messages and phone calls followed, and we agreed to meet up at 2pm on Monday 26 January – a date I remember so well. I was nervous and spent ages figuring out what to wear. Graham had suggested that we could go for a walk, so my outfit needed to be sexy, yet comfortable and practical. Eventually I chose a pair of skinny jeans and boots with a comfy jumper, and drove to Graham's house. Luckily I found it easily, and was immediately impressed by the beautiful cottage that I saw before me; quirky and well kept, with bags of Somerset character.

I walked up the short path and closed the gate behind me. The front door opened sharply; Graham had been waiting on the other side, having watched me getting out of my car through his window – talk about keen! The cottage was as beautiful inside as out, impeccably clean and with a wood burner to warm us.

We decided to go for a walk in the woods nearby and jumped into Graham's gorgeous BMW Convertible to whisk us there. As we walked our hands kept brushing against each other, but neither of us knew what to do about it! I knew right away that I really liked him. It was so easy to chat to him and we talked freely, discussing the people we knew, what we'd been up to since school, and our memories from the time when we'd known each other. He made me laugh and was a proper gentleman; not the sort of guy that I'd normally have gone for! The afternoon was lovely and we went back to his for a hot chocolate and a sit-down with a film. Graham put his arm around me and we snuggled on the sofa to watch it; it was the perfect end to a brilliant first date.

Over the next few days the West Country was hit by some of the worst snow that any of us had seen for some time, making travelling almost impossible. The thought of being snowed in alone filled me with dread. I rang Graham to see what the snow was like near him. When he replied that it was pretty awful there too, I informed him that I was dropping everything and heading over!

The roads were the worst I'd ever seen, and just as I was making my way round the last corner before Graham's house, the car skidded and I came to a stop right in the middle of a junction. Dressed in my wellies and thick winter coat I walked the last hundred yards or so to Graham's house. He and his neighbour hurried off to rescue my car with a shovel, and once it was safely parked outside the house Graham and I made our way inside for what turned out to be five days of being snowed in together. We had the most amazing time, larking about in the fresh white snow, watching films together, and getting to know each other.

I already knew that this was the man I wanted to spend the rest of my life with.

Chapter Two

Over the next few weeks Graham and I saw each other at every opportunity. It all felt too good to be true – I was falling for him in a big way, and quickly. At that time I was due to go on holiday with my family to celebrate my dad's 60th birthday but the thought of spending time away from Graham was almost too much to bear.

One morning I was taking a bath when I found a strange lump in my right breast. It was the size of a pea, and definitely not something I had felt before. I had undergone breast reduction surgery three years previously and was at first quite certain that it was related – perhaps a stitch that had not dissolved properly, or a lump of scar tissue. On closer inspection, though, I realised that the lump was in an area that hadn't been stitched. In that moment, and without any idea why, I was very concerned.

I made a mental note to call the doctor as soon as the surgery opened on Monday morning. The lump played on my mind all day though so, when I got home that evening, I texted Graham in the hopes of offloading some of my worry. His auntie had died of breast cancer and he had previously been involved with a girl who had sadly died from ovarian cancer, so he quite rightly insisted that I get everything checked out just to be safe.

As soon as I could, I made myself a doctor's appointment and headed to the surgery with trepidation. My GP was a lovely man, and, although he was endlessly reassuring, he took the lump seriously, advising me to monitor it for a week in case it was connected to my monthly cycle or other hormonal changes. If it was still there the following week I was to return without delay and I'd be referred for further tests.

Later that week I was due to fly to Goa for my dad's birthday trip. While I knew I was going to miss Graham terribly, I knew it would be good to have a distraction from my worry. I hadn't told anyone else about the lump – it seemed unnecessary to worry them in the run up to our holiday.

The first day of our holiday arrived. The thought of leaving Graham was gut-wrenching – we had been together just seven weeks, but our feet hadn't yet had time to touch the ground. We were falling head over heels in love with each other at breakneck speed.

With my dad's celebrations and thoughts of Graham whizzing through my mind I reluctantly boarded the plane. During the holiday Graham and I kept in constant contact with each other, but it was hard not having him there with me – especially as he was the only one who knew about my lump. I eventually confided in my mum and her friend, and they did their best to reassure me despite their concern. Mum's best friend's son was battling cancer at the time and, aged just 40, the prognosis didn't look good at all for him. It was so hard to see someone we cared about facing such a terrible illness.

That week couldn't go quickly enough, and I was beside myself with excitement as we headed home. I couldn't wait to touch down in Gatwick, and rang Graham as soon as we landed. We promised that we would never spend a moment away from each other again – it was all very dramatic, but felt so right. Bright and early the next day, I headed for Graham's – he had just moved and I couldn't wait to be his first houseguest. Seeing him again was fantastic and I realised there and then that I never wanted to be away from this man again. He looked more gorgeous than ever and we couldn't stop holding each other.

That afternoon we headed into town. Graham had some errands to run and we decided to enjoy lunch together while we were out. I remember that afternoon as though it were yesterday; we walked through Exeter's main shopping centre, holding hands and chatting, until suddenly Graham stopped.

'I need to go in there,' he said, pointing in the direction of a jewellers' shop on the High Street. I asked him what he needed to go in there for and he began to look nervous.

'A ring.' My mind started racing.

'A ring? What sort of ring?'

'An engagement ring.' It took a moment for Graham's words to sink in, yet nothing before had ever felt so right. So we went into the jewellers, hand in hand, and chose a beautiful engagement ring. In that moment I couldn't have been happier – we were on cloud nine, and I finally felt as if my life was heading in the right direction.

Chapter Three

Two days after Graham had proposed, we decided to go and have a look around a few wedding dress shops; I just couldn't help myself! We wanted to get married as soon as possible and, although I am a traditionalist in many ways, I've always believed that the groom's opinion is important when choosing a wedding dress. After all, it was Graham that I was trying to impress! As we browsed a rack of beautiful dresses there was a small piece of fabric that seemed to stand out from the gowns around it. Although there can't have been more than five inches of material on show, Graham and I had both reached for the same dress. I already knew that this was The One. Trying the dress on only confirmed my suspicions; it fitted perfectly and looked absolutely stunning.

Despite all our excitement, I still had the lump in my right breast. I was due to go and see the specialist the next day and didn't feel like we could really celebrate our engagement until we knew that it was nothing.

The day of my appointment came. I remember sitting in the waiting room with Graham and being surprised by just how many young people were there with me. You think of cancer being an old person's disease, or something that strikes those who lead unhealthy lives, yet here we all were.

I was called into the room, and instinctively told Graham to wait outside, but the nurse was very insistent that he come in with me, and it was then that the nerves really began to creep in. We waited for the specialist to enter, becoming more and more anxious as the minutes ticked by. He was a lovely gentleman and gave me time to explain what had been going on and what I had discovered in my breast. As I sat on the couch being poked and prodded the room went eerily silent, and I couldn't help but worry. After what seemed liked ages, the specialist explained that he wanted to take a biopsy, and I agreed; at that point I was willing to undergo any test to try and relieve the worry.

Preparing me for the biopsy, the specialist described the process in detail; usually, when a needle is inserted into a cyst, it will draw fluid. If no fluid is present, the lump could be something more sinister. It was painful as the thick needle went in, and the sound of the machine collecting its sample was like a staple gun. Graham and I held our breaths as the needle was retracted; there was no fluid.

The specialist explained that, while things weren't looking good, he would send off the needle and biopsy sample to be completely sure. We were now faced with an agonising, week-long wait for the results. Even then, as we left the specialist's office, I don't think I expected the lump to be anything serious, despite having had a lifelong belief that I would one day be diagnosed with breast cancer. There was no reason for that overwhelming fear, yet it had always been there. Even so, I didn't believe that the time was now.

The week dragged, until finally we found ourselves in that waiting room again. This time I studied the faces of those around me, absorbing their fear.

We were called into the specialist's office and, with little time to pause for breath, he said, 'You have HER2 positive breast cancer.' I had no idea what that meant, and the words swam around my head. Graham and I were then ushered into another room to discuss the plan of action. At this stage the doctors didn't know anything about my cancer – simply that I had it.

We left the room with a wealth of information to take away and digest, and a plan to return for surgery to remove the lump within the next couple of weeks. At this point I still hadn't cried. Graham's face was ashen with shock. We'd been together for just eight weeks and were now faced with the prospect that I could die; this wasn't the plan.

As we left the hospital I rang my mum to deliver the news. It was only then that I broke down. I was as devastated for my family as I was for myself. We made our way to the car and I tried to be as matter-of-fact about it as I could be, joking about losing my hair. I knew that I was going to put up one heck of a fight, but was scared of what the treatment would be like. At the time I didn't even know what chemo-therapy was, other than that it made you really, really sick.

After telling my family I decided to take the huge leap of telling my friends and acquaintances through Facebook. I didn't want to risk the awkwardness of bumping into people and having to tell them, or finding out they knew from someone else. I needed to be in control of my illness, including which people knew and how. Again I made a joke of my diagnosis, lamenting the future loss of my hair.

That night I went to bed and sobbed my heart out. I lay there and pretended to be in a coffin, wondering what it would be like and how it would feel to just slip away. Is there a heaven? Would I get to go there? After two hours or more of crying I slipped off into a deep sleep.

* * *

When I woke up the next day I decided that I had shed the last of my tears. I was determined to fight cancer with every bone in my body. Over the next few weeks I focused on enjoying life and appreciating everything around me. I spent hours playing with my hair, went on a big night out with friends for what would be the last time in a while, and planned as much as I could to make the next six months of chemotherapy as easy as possible.

Unfortunately my job with the council was no longer secure, and it looked as if I was going to be made redundant in the very near future. I wasn't sure if this was good or bad timing! Luckily I had racked up an awful lot of owed holiday and lieu days, and hoped that the money would tide me over for a few months until I knew how hard the chemo was going to hit me. I couldn't continue my wedding planning either, so I passed my workload onto a friend; it wouldn't have been fair on the couples to put any less than my all into their weddings. Our own wedding was going to have to take a back seat for now, but I used the photo that Graham had taken of me in The Dress as my inspiration to keep going. I was determined to wear it one day.

My surgery went without a hitch and they removed the lump with clear margins; they were able to cut around the tumour and leave cancer-free tissue behind. The surgeons also removed nineteen of my lymph nodes. Luckily, they revealed, the disease had been contained; the doctors were happy that my cancer had not spread. At last, my first piece of good news since the diagnosis!

Chemotherapy was decided upon as the next course of action, and was due to take place over the next six months. It all seemed so overwhelming, and so fast moving. When the swelling from my operation eventually went down I was left with a concave in my right breast – yet another war wound to add to my already burgeoning collection of scars! I often joked that I looked like a completed dot-to-dot, and used humour to help me through some of my toughest days.

By now it was the end of May and Graham's 30th birthday was fast approaching. It was going to be the first birthday we would celebrate as a couple and, although I knew he expected it to be a quiet affair, I had a few tricks up my sleeve to make it amazing for him; not least the surprise birthday party I had planned! Organising the party hadn't been the easiest of tasks, as although I had heard all about his family members I was yet to meet many of them. However, with the help of Facebook and his mum, the invites were sent in plenty of time.

I'd decided to hold the party at Graham's house and, while he was at work, prepared all the food and decorated his lounge with balloons, banners and streamers. I told him that I had a surprise for him;

he was to go off to work as normal, taking a change of clothes with him, and then meet me on the other side of Exeter in a pub. The plan was set! As we enjoyed our drinks, members of Graham's family and friends began to fill his house – I have no idea to this day how I managed to keep the secret.

When it was time to leave, I handed Graham a blindfold and instructed him to put it on. We set off on our journey, taking a long-winded route to try and throw him off the scent. We must have explored the whole of Exeter that night, travelling up and down roads that I never even knew existed in an attempt to disorientate Graham. Unfortunately, as we neared his house, a train sounded its horn and alerted Graham to the fact that we were nearing home; I started to panic a little. Nevertheless, I carried on up the steep hill leading to his house. He drove that road so often that he knew every lump and dip; I was sure he was onto me.

We made our way through Graham's front door and upstairs, past the living room where everyone was hiding. How he didn't hear their hushed whispers and giggles I'll never know! I whipped off the blindfold at last, just in time for the room to erupt into cheers and birthday congratulations. It was a lovely moment, and I will never forget his face as he drank in the sight before him. I was so grateful that his family and friends had turned out in force to give Graham a reason to smile.

Graham's grandparents were there too – his granddad, who he affectionately called Gramps, had been ill for some time, but Graham and I were unprepared for the deterioration in his health. His face was grey and riddled with pain, and he didn't move from his chair all night. The family knew that he was suffering from cancer, but not to what extent. He was a proud man, not wanting to make a fuss, and an amazing husband to Graham's grandma.

In the two months leading up to Graham's birthday, Gramps had made the decision that he and his wife should move into a home together. We all knew that he was making plans for the future, ensuring that Graham's grandma would be safe. It was heartbreaking. As they left the party, Gramps said goodbye to each family member individually, as though he knew that this was going to be the last time he saw everyone. He was unable to make his way down the stairs, so Graham carried him out to the car. He later confided that he'd had an overwhelming urge to tell Gramps that he loved him, something that he hadn't done throughout his adult years.

The following week Graham and I travelled to London to catch a show. Visiting the West End had been on my 'bucket list', and a friend had kindly purchased the tickets as a special treat for my impending birthday. While packing up ready to leave for a short day of sightseeing before returning home, we got a call from Graham's mum. Gramps had taken a turn for the worse. Graham was visibly upset and I made the decision to leave there and then. As we pulled up at the nursing home, the doctor was just leaving. Graham shot out of the car.

'How is he?' Graham asked. The doctor's face was grave.

'I'm sorry. He passed away about ten minutes ago.' We had missed Gramps by minutes; it was devastating. He had been such a character and, although I hadn't known the family for very long, he already had a special place in my heart.

Chapter Four

It was decided that I would start chemotherapy as soon as possible. Gramps's funeral was drawing closer and had been planned around my treatment, giving me a day or two to recover from my first dose. It had been good for cancer to not be at the forefront of my mind; supporting Graham and his family had been my primary concern.

Chemotherapy can ruin your chances of having children. As there was no time to freeze my eggs, the doctors had suggested putting my ovaries to sleep to try and protect them. There was no guarantee that it would work, but Graham and I both thought that it was worth a try. I knew that I needed to come to terms with the fact that we would probably never be able to have children of our own, but, at that very moment, all I wanted was to beat cancer.

Before the chemotherapy could be administered I had a small operation to insert a portacath. This device, which looked very much like a Flying Saucer sherbet penny sweet, fitted snugly onto my ribcage and was connected to my heart via a long tube that would dispense the chemotherapy intravenously. I was so nervous about starting my treatment, not least because I knew there was a good chance it would make me sick. No one particularly likes being sick, but I am terrible at coping with it; I can't even hear someone vomiting without crying and freaking out a little.

The nurses were lovely, but, as they handled the bags of chemotherapy drugs, they resembled something out of a Hollywood chemical disaster movie. They had to wear protective overalls and huge, armpit-length rubber gloves and protective goggles; not exactly reassuring! I will never forget the feeling as they linked the bag of chemotherapy up to my portacath. I knew that the fluid now seeping into my body was poison and that, even if I'd asked them to stop there and then, my hair would still have fallen out. Deep down, I was heartbroken.

The treatment took around three hours to complete and I went home later that day. Although I felt tired, I was relieved that there was no sickness. All of the research that I'd done had led me to believe that the sickness would eventually catch up with me, but I felt fine the next day. I started to feel positive for the first time since my diagnosis – perhaps I was going to breeze through this after all.

* * *

No Ordinary Wedding Planner

Gramps's funeral took place a couple of days after my first dose of chemotherapy. It was a beautiful service, and I was so proud of Graham as I watched him carry his granddad's coffin into the crematorium. Death now had a weird new meaning to me – a sort of realness that hadn't existed before.

It wasn't long before my next session was due. It was relentless. As the levels of chemotherapy drugs built up in my body, I began to feel weaker and more tired. I was still lucky as I was never sick, although I wasn't entirely surprised with the amount of anti-sickness medication that I was on.

A few weeks into my treatment, Mum joined me for my latest dose. During the session she received a phone call to say that her best friend's son, who had also been fighting cancer, had passed away. Mum had known Brian since he was a young lad, and was absolutely devastated. I knew that my cancer diagnosis had been very hard on her, and that this awful news would now make it that little bit more real.

In that moment, I couldn't possibly have known that Brian's death was about to become the beginning of a pattern. As a cancer patient you meet many other people along the way who are sharing your journey. The more involved you get the more heartache you experience, and I found myself attending so many funerals. It never gets any easier, despite the frequency with which bad news comes around – if anything it gets harder.

Chapter Five

With every session of chemotherapy, things got tougher and tougher. When I got home I would put myself straight to bed and sleep, although I'd return to feeling almost normal again a few short hours later. My treatment was always on a Tuesday and I remember the fear that washed over me whenever someone mentioned that day – my tummy would do somersaults, and I would completely fill with dread. The drugs used during my chemotherapy were bright red and I found that I grew to detest the colour. Anything red repulsed me. I couldn't bear to be in the same room as anything that resembled those drugs.

As the days after my treatment went on, I would improve a little and then relapse significantly. The effect that the chemotherapy had on my moods was severe, and I know I was a horrible person to be around! I was angry at my situation, and feeling awful never helps matters; it just envelops you and leaves little room for rational thought.

Another side effect of my treatment was an increased appetite. There were Saturday nights when Graham and I would order pizza and sit in front of *The X-Factor*, comfortably eating more than enough food for four or more people; and yet, five minutes later, I could have eaten the whole meal again. I would experience horrible pains in my chest, like severe indigestion, and the only way to relieve them was to eat. I knew my weight was creeping up and I began to feel really uncomfortable about myself.

I'd let my hair fall out naturally, and one weekend caught a glimpse of myself in the mirror. I had no idea how thin my hair had got; from the back, I looked like a monk! It was then that I decided to shave it off, giving myself a little control over my cancer. I was also fed up of finding hair all over my home and clothes, so I took a razor to my head the next time I found myself alone. Within minutes there was nothing left. It was a weird feeling, slightly liberating, and there were no tears. I'd just accepted losing my hair as part of the process, and decided to post a photo on Facebook to let people know I was okay. Within seconds of uploading the photo of myself smiling, I was inundated with comments – I knew I had the support I needed to keep fighting.

* * *

Naomi Thomas

I was due to meet Graham that night for a drink and, other than on Facebook, he was yet to see my new look. I donned the long, blonde wig that I had chosen a few weeks before and set off to meet him, slightly nervous about how he'd react. I arrived feeling emotional and angry at the whole situation, and as soon as I saw Graham I was overcome with anxiety and shame for having no hair. We had barely been together for five months and now Graham was having to face all of this with me; it seemed so unfair on both of us. I wanted to give Graham the opportunity to walk away, as much as it hurt me to do so.

I explained how I felt to Graham. He hugged me close and pulled off my wig, drawing me into a deep and meaningful kiss. We pulled apart and he looked into my eyes.

'I'm not going anywhere,' he said, and I knew that he meant it.

That weekend the pain in my chest peaked. I had become so depressed that I told Graham I didn't want to live any more. I became hysterical as he insisted that he was taking me to the hospital. The only way he could get me into the car was to promise me that he wouldn't leave me there, and that we could come home that night. I knew that he was just worried for me; I was in such a bad place that he had no way of knowing what I would do to myself.

No Ordinary Wedding Planner

We arrived at the hospital and went straight to the oncology ward. The doctor came to meet us and asked to see all the medication that I was on, which Graham dutifully emptied out in front of him. The doctor explained that half the medications I had been using should not be taken together, and that this was probably the cause of my erratic thoughts and chest pains. As soon as we got my medications sorted, the doctors allowed me to go home. Graham watched me like a hawk from then on, but I soon started to feel so much better in myself.

With no hair and my ever-increasing weight I couldn't feel good about myself at all. My clothes were pretty and feminine but just didn't look right with a bald head. I was trying to wear my wig as much as possible, but it was the height of summer and far too hot. I knew that I didn't have to wear it, but didn't want to embarrass anyone that I came across while I was out; I wore the wig for them. On occasions that thought made me angry. Looking back it was a stupid way to feel, but I couldn't help it. I remember sitting in a restaurant one evening with Graham, the sweat dripping from inside my wig and down my back. He repeatedly told me to take it off, but I just couldn't – I'd walked in wearing it, what would people say if I took it off? I endured the rest of the meal with it on, but inside I was seething.

* * *

As the months went by and the end of my chemo-therapy came into sight, I realised that I was begin-ning to run out of savings very rapidly. Money was getting tighter and tighter, and I didn't know how much longer I could afford to keep a roof over my head. I hadn't wanted to rush into moving in with Graham, but it was looking as though it was the only option for both of us. Graham worked selling second-hand cars, but the Government's scrappage scheme had put paid to much of his income. Cars that he would normally have bought were being scrapped, and his earnings were dwindling to noth-ing. There were times when he had to decide whether to drive to work and try to earn money, or eat.

Graham always chose to work, and I would find him living off a loaf of bread, eating toast for his tea. Living in Devon was becoming increasingly expen-sive, and we had discussed moving to Nottinghamshire to be closer to some of our family, namely Graham's dad, and my nan, aunty and uncle. My aunty in particular had been an absolute rock to me during my treatment, sending cards and flowers to cheer me up. She never forgot an appointment, always wished me luck, and touched base after every session to check I was okay – words cannot express how grate-ful I will always be to her. My nan, well into her 80s, was funny and loving and always talked sense. I knew that my family had kept much of my illness from her, but she knew exactly what was going on!

No Ordinary Wedding Planner

Graham and I decided it was time to think about the big move. The Nottinghamshire area was cheaper in terms of living costs, and it would mean we could spend time with family we'd not been local to for a long time. My nan's age and health were also at the forefront of my decision, and I was eager to spend as much time with her as possible before it was too late. Our minds were set.

Chapter Six

We decided to move as soon as possible, giving us time to get back on our feet. We also had high hopes of returning to the West Country in the future; it was our home, after all. Graham and I found a house and, while it didn't tick all of our boxes, it was much cheaper than the houses we currently lived in, and much bigger too. It was in Bilsthorpe, a village about 14 miles north of Nottingham, 20 minutes from Graham's dad, and 45 minutes from my family in Sheffield. It suited us perfectly.

We had also heard good things about the local oncology department, so I knew I was in safe hands for the remainder of my treatment. My chemotherapy was now coming to an end and my oncologist had suggested that I should also have six weeks of radiotherapy to ensure that the cancer was well and truly beaten. That would involve targeting a beam of radiation at the area where my lump had been, from Monday to Friday for the whole six weeks; still, if it would help in the long run I was prepared to endure the treatment.

We quickly signed for the house and moved in at the beginning of December. Although it wasn't our dream house the extra room was most welcome, and the location was lovely. It was lovely to finally be alone. Our wonderful friend, Stuart, helped us to move our stuff, and before long we were settled in.

I soon started my radiotherapy treatment, and came out the other side unscathed, with no real lasting side effects. I felt as though I had come to the end of a long journey, and attended my next oncology appointment in the hope that everything was finally over, and that I would be sent on my way with an 'I kicked cancer's butt' badge for posterity!

At the appointment I met a lovely consultant called Dr Khan. She had a really caring nature and I warmed to her immediately. She informed me that the plan was for me to start taking Herceptin and Tamoxifen, two drugs that acted as hormone blockers. Being HER2 positive meant that my cancer fed off the oestrogen in my body; taking these new drugs would remove the hormone and essentially starve any potential cancer cells, stopping them before they could form.

I'd done my own research, though, and knew that if I started this new course of treatment it would be another five years (at least) before I was completely drug-free. That was five long years before Graham and I could start thinking about having a baby. I knew that getting pregnant would be a long shot, but if there was any chance at all then we wanted to take it. How many more precautions were they expecting me to take? After all, my cancer had been eliminated as soon as the lump had been removed. I didn't want to be ungrateful – I knew that these drugs were very special, helping to save lives all over the country, so I didn't make the decision not to take them lightly.

It was nearly Christmas, our first as a couple in a new home together, and we were turning it into a cosy love nest for us to enjoy over the festive period. I couldn't wait to close out the world and just chill out together. We had invited Graham's mum and grandma to stay with us over Christmas and enjoyed a lovely few days with them, eating plenty and playing family games of Trivial Pursuit. I had Grandma on my team, and even at the age of 90 she helped me storm to victory against Graham and his mum.

New Year's Eve arrived and I realised then just how much my life had changed in just 12 months. A year before I had been getting ready to go out and dance the night away, and now I was celebrating with a wonderful man who loved me more than I'd ever been loved before (and vice versa). I'd fought cancer and won! Wow, what a reason to celebrate. Not knowing anyone locally we decided to stay in, cracking open a few bottles with the intention of having an early night. As usual, though, things didn't turn out as planned. Graham and I drank our combined body weight in alcohol, danced with the Christmas tree, fell over lots, and got to bed in the early hours. It was a great way to spend New Year's Eve; we had turned over the page onto a new chapter of our lives.

Chapter Seven

The only reminders of my previous year from hell were my bald head and the portacath device still embedded in my chest. I had decided that it was time for the portacath to go, and was booked in for a minor procedure under general anaesthetic to have it removed. Yet more scars to add to my never-ending dot-to-dot!

We arrived at the day surgery only to discover that they didn't seem to be expecting me. They sent us to the waiting room, but a few hours later we were still there, although many of the other patients had now been and gone. We went to check that we hadn't been forgotten about, only to find that it seemed we had. The secretary to the surgeon had initially rung to offer me the appointment, and then forgotten to tell the surgeon that he'd need to book the theatre slot. Being the impatient, feisty soul that I am, I'm afraid I got a little vocal – I call it 'getting things done', while Graham refers to it as 'kicking off'. Whatever you want to call it, it was now 2pm and I was starving. The surgeon agreed to do my procedure if no urgent admissions came in, and asked the nurses to prep me for surgery. By then my stomach thought my throat had been cut.

The nurse was extremely apologetic about what had happened, and completed the necessary paperwork and pregnancy test, which is standard procedure prior to any operation. A few moments later she walked back into the room with a huge smile on her face. She held out her hand in front of me, clutching the pregnancy test that I'd just done. Within seconds my mind and heart were racing; I couldn't be ... could I? I looked up at the nurse, whose face said it all.

'Oh my God!' I squealed. I was going to be a mum; my life had changed yet again in a split second. The nurse gave me a huge hug and told me that she had never had that happen in a pre-op assessment before. Graham was still sitting in the waiting room, completely oblivious to this news. 'I'll send him in,' the nurse said, reading my mind. I had just seconds to decide how I would break this news to Graham. He was going to be a daddy!

Graham walked into the room and asked me if I was okay. Doing my best to keep a straight face, I held out the pregnancy test in my hand, just as the nurse had done a few moments before. His reaction was much the same as mine, and I'm sure the lady in the cubicle next to us must have thought we were mad. We were both on cloud nine; we had been trying for a baby for just one month and our wildest dreams had come true.

The positive pregnancy test meant that my portacath removal had to be carried out by local anaesthetic, but the surgeon and his team were in such good spirits in the operating theatre when they heard our news. They all crowded around, asking if we had known that I was pregnant and what we would call the baby. Graham and I finally felt as though we were being rewarded for the year of hell that we'd just endured. By October we would have a baby, our very own bundle of joy, here with us.

Or would we? My happiness soon turned to anxiety as I imagined all the things that could go wrong. I'd only just finished chemotherapy and radiotherapy, and surely it would still be travelling round my body. What if it harmed our unborn child?

My pregnancy was confirmed for us a couple of weeks later. We rang our parents to tell them the good news; they were thrilled, although slightly nervous too. Our midwife arranged for us to see a specialist, and for me to be under their care for the duration of the pregnancy. Although we had the baby's wellbeing hanging over our heads, we had instantly fallen in love with the idea of being parents, and couldn't help planning things and getting excited about every milestone. To have that taken away would have been devastating.

As my pregnancy progressed I loved seeing my tummy change, and knowing that I was carrying a new life was one of the best feelings in the world. The day before our 12-week scan, though, I noticed I was bleeding during a trip to the toilet. I panicked immediately, and as I lay on the bed in the scan room I was prepared for the worst. All of a sudden the baby's heartbeat was on the screen, pumping loud and clear for Graham and me to hear. Our baby was fine; its weight, length and heartbeat were all perfect. The sonographer explained that we'd know more at our 20-week scan; that was the most crucial, along with the results of the Downs screening test, but as far as we could tell everything was fine. The relief was immense and we both broke down in tears of joy.

The Downs screening results came back normal, and as we approached the 20-week scan we were beside ourselves with excitement. I was adamant that we were having a boy, although I didn't care as long as we had a healthy baby.

As I lay down for the scan I was still convinced that our baby was a boy, but the only person who could tell us for certain was currently slopping cold jelly all over my ballooning stomach. The room was silent as he negotiated my bump, searching for the baby's position. There it was again, the beautiful sound of our baby's heartbeat. The sonographer asked us what we thought we were having. I immediately piped up with my theory.

'You'd be right, it's a boy!' he confirmed.

So there he was. Our little boy, who was to be named Devon. It was a name that I had fallen in love with about six years previously when the celebrity Nell McAndrew had chosen it for her baby boy. Luckily Graham liked the name too, although his mum's face said it all when we told her. It suited our son from the moment he was born.

With everything going right in our lives once again, we began to talk about setting a date for the wedding. We knew that we'd have to move quickly, and so went to see some venues. One particular place that struck a chord was a beautiful Italian-inspired hotel in the heart of Birmingham. They were able to offer us a really good deal, and so we set a date for the following August Bank Holiday; finally we could start getting excited about what lay ahead. We knew this meant that our little boy would be with us on our special day – maybe the events of the past few months had happened for a reason.

* * *

Not long after the 20-week scan my back began to hurt. The pain was centred around the top of my back where my shoulders met, and I was finding it increasingly difficult to get comfy in a chair or bed. As time passed the pain got worse and worse, and I got in touch with the midwife to see what could be done. She put me on the waiting list for physiotherapy, and thought that the pain was probably caused by the extra weight of the baby that I was carrying around. No matter what I did, nothing eased my back at all. It got to the point where I was spending much of my time in bed and I'd become a Deep Heat addict, spraying it on liberally at every opportunity until I became immune to its effects.

During that time I went to Devon to see my parents for a few days. By this point I was really beginning to struggle and had been given Codeine to take sparingly when needed. Secretly, though, I was taking about four times the recommended dose. I'd reached such a low point that I didn't care what happened to me, or the baby, as long as the pain went away. My mum booked a session of acupuncture for me. It wasn't something we were big believers in, but right then I'd have tried standing on my head while doing the Hula if you had told me it would help. It helped for a few days, but soon the intense pain was back.

* * *

At around 30 weeks pregnant it was discovered that I had gestational diabetes. My diet was pretty good, so I wasn't able to control the diabetes through changing what I ate, and the tablets that I was prescribed didn't seem to help either. The next step would be insulin injections, which I really wasn't keen on. Luckily, we never got that far as it was discovered Devon was breech; the chances were I'd be having him early. I was so pleased, as I couldn't cope with the pain in my back any longer. By 34 weeks I was having to stay at home much of the time, and needed to be pushed in a wheelchair when I did manage to get out.

All I wanted was to have my baby, hopefully relieving the pressure in my back. I'd been begging the doctors for a C-section as early as possible. It was eventually decided that Devon would be delivered at 38 weeks by C-section, unless anything changed in the meantime.

One evening, just before our planned birth, Graham and I had decided to go to the cinema; it was one last night out, just the two of us, before Devon changed our lives for ever.

During the film, I found myself fidgeting in my seat. I just couldn't get comfortable and, as the credits rolled, I went to stand but found I couldn't. My back felt as though it had completely seized up. I grabbed Graham's arm in a panic and he knew immediately that something wasn't right. We waited until the auditorium had emptied and then Graham tried to lift me. The pain was excruciating. I had managed to stand up by now, but was huddled over, unable to straighten up or move my legs to walk.

It took 45 minutes for me to shuffle out of the cinema, with Graham helping me into the car. He drove me straight to the hospital, where I was admitted and told that I would be there until the baby was born. This was not how I imagined spending the week before I became a mum! There was so much to do at home, including prepping the nursery and washing baby clothes, and now Graham had been lumbered with it all as well as keeping me company. I was just thankful that our son would soon be with us, and was hoping that the pain would subside at last. He was still in the breech position, so my C-section was planned for Friday that week; at last, a date!

The night before the C-section Graham said goodbye at 8pm as visiting hours finished. I waved to him as he got into the car. After all that had happened, we were finally at the end of a long and difficult pregnancy, about to become parents!

Chapter Eight

The next morning Graham and I made our way to theatre. As I was wheeled in the song by Simon Webbe, 'No Worries', came on the radio. I recall hearing the lyrics, 'I just know your life's gonna change,' floating above any other noise in that busy room, and feeling as though the whole thing had been planned. By now, I was feeling really nervous. The doctors and nurses bustled around me, erecting the screen that would shield me from the procedure I was about to endure. The care we received that day was superb, and the staff made us feel as though ours was the first baby to ever be born there – it was lovely.

I couldn't feel anything and looked towards Graham, waiting for his face to show any signs of something happening. Though under the effects of the epidural, I was sure that I was shaking with fear, excitement and adrenalin. After a few moments, and lots of tugging and pushing down, which felt like someone clambering about on my chest, the doctor announced that our baby had been born. Graham's face lit up. However, there was no sound to be heard from our new baby son. Weren't babies meant to cry when they were born? Panic began to wash over me. I looked up at Graham, who was transfixed by what was going on. Just as I began to speak our little boy let out a small cry, like a lamb. I burst into tears of relief and happiness.

Devon Joel Thomas was born on 23 September 2010, weighing 7lb 9½ oz. He was soon wrapped up and brought over to Graham for his first cuddle. Seeing his little face and one tiny hand poking up through the towel was the most amazing moment of my life; I felt complete, and loved him more than anything else in the world.

As I was still numb, all I could do was look at him. I was so desperate for that first cuddle. The nurse took Devon and his daddy over to the weighing station to take his measurements, at which point my son peed all over the nurse, not once, but twice in quick succession. What an entrance!

Half an hour or so later Devon was laid in my arms for the first time. Tears began to flow as I was wheeled into a little side room, and we were left alone together. Within minutes Devon was having his first feed. Breastfeeding meant the world to me, but with all that I'd been through the doctors couldn't be sure that I would be able to feed. But here I was, and Devon had taken to it right away. I felt as though I could finally do something for my baby all by myself – it was an amazing feeling.

Graham's dad was our first visitor, bringing with him a small blue teddy bear, Bed Time Bear, which Devon still sleeps with to this day. We placed his first gift at the end of his cot and I lay transfixed, hardly daring to believe that we'd created this new life against all odds.

That night, when Graham left for home, I knew that he was really torn about leaving us. It was going to be very difficult for me to care for a newborn during the night, and it has always annoyed me that new dads are sent home alone after such an incredible day. Devon and I stood at the window and waved his daddy off. What a day! If I had thought that the day's events had been hard work, then I was in for a shock.

Devon was a very relaxed baby, unlike the newborn across the ward. Every time it cried Devon would begin to scream too, and I didn't sleep a wink all night. The next morning I told the nursing staff that I wanted to go home, despite being due to remain in hospital for five more days. I was relieved when they agreed to let me go.

After packing everything up, Graham brought in Devon's new car seat. We strapped our newborn son in and were struck by how tiny and fragile he looked. I was still on crutches, although I could feel that the pain in my back was easing slightly. Graham now had two of us to look after and was going to have his hands full for a while. He rose to the challenge brilliantly, though, and I couldn't have been prouder of him. That day, Graham drove the slowest I'd ever seen him drive. After all, we were carrying a precious load this time.

Chapter Nine

We'd barely had time to settle in before people began arriving to see the newest member of the family. It was pretty overwhelming, to be honest, especially as I still wasn't feeling 100 per cent. All I wanted to do was bond with my baby, and for us to get to know each other as a family, but everyone was desperate to meet Devon.

I was still unable to get around without crutches, even though the pain had eased a little. This meant that I couldn't stand to rock my son, or push his pram – the few things I had been dreaming about doing my whole life.

Although nothing prepares you for having your own child we were soon starting to get into a routine of feeds and nappy changes. I'd worked with children since the age of 19 and so certainly wasn't a novice, but I questioned everything that I was doing for Devon. I just wanted the best for him, and could never have prepared myself for the love and protectiveness I felt for this new little person. Even though my pregnancy had been horrendous, having Devon in my arms made it all worthwhile.

During this time we were told Devon had a problem with his hips. As his hip joints had failed to form properly he would need to wear a harness for the first 12 weeks of his life to give them a chance to grow and develop. This meant that his little legs would be spread akimbo so that he couldn't move them. Graham was devastated at the thought of him not being perfect, but I was just so thankful there was a good chance of correcting the problem. My chemotherapy and radiotherapy had not affected him in any way.

One afternoon, just six days after Devon's birth, we had gone into town to get some shopping. October was approaching and the weather had turned a little chilly. By the time we got home I was feeling horrendous and, no matter how close I sat to our electric fire, I just couldn't get warm. I decided to go upstairs and have a sleep to see if I could shake off the shivery feeling. When I finally got to the top of the stairs, taking one step at a time and supporting myself with the crutches, I began to shake violently. An uncontrollable wave flooded over me, and I shouted at Graham to come quickly. He shot to my side and was terrified to see that my lips had gone blue. He helped me to lie down on the bed, leaning my crutches against the wall.

Graham checked me over and said that he thought I had a temperature. He decided that if I was no better after an hour we would head to hospital. But I had no desire to go back there. Filled with determination, I decided I was feeling well enough to get up again just half an hour later. As I leaned forward to sit up, an electric shock rippled down my back and into my right leg; it was perhaps the worst pain I had ever felt in my life. I screamed in agony. The more I tensed or moved, the stronger the shocks came. By now Graham was by my side, but he was powerless to stop the pain. With his help I shuffled to the edge of the bed and lifted myself up on the crutches to see if being off my spine relieved the pressure at all. It didn't; the shocks kept coming thick and fast, and by now I was screaming blue murder.

Graham grabbed the phone and called for the doctor, who said he would get to us as soon as he could, but had still not appeared half an hour later. In the meantime I had tried to sit down, only to discover that my body would no longer bend in the right places; it was as if my brain wasn't telling my body what to do. I stood, near crippled, on my crutches and sobbed. A second phone call to the doctor revealed that he had been held up and wouldn't be with us at any point soon. I was furious – I knew my body and this was so much more than back pain.

With Graham now crying, Devon screaming, and me sobbing my heart out, the decision was made to call 999, and we were relieved to know that help would soon be on its way. Half an hour later, though, the ambulance still wasn't with us. We were all so distressed, and I begged Graham to call 999 again. An hour had passed by the time the ambulance arrived. I was relieved that we finally had medical professionals to help, but was also distressed that we'd been left so long. Why was no one taking my pain seriously?

The paramedics offered me some gas and air to ease the pain, which didn't work. They then decided to administer morphine to see if my muscles would relax enough for the spasms to stop, but after the maximum dose they could give me I still felt no better, the disabling feeling as strong as ever. At this point the ambulance driver gave me my options; there was no doubt about it, I was going to hospital. The only way I was going to get there was if the fire brigade was called to come and assist, or if the air ambulance was summoned and winched me out of the bedroom window. I still couldn't move my legs, sit, or lie down, so I didn't care who came as long as they were quick. Although they weren't legally obliged to attend for a back problem, the fire brigade agreed to come. Within minutes we heard the fire engine coming and saw the reflection of its blue lights on the houses around us.

Our poor neighbours must have wondered what the hell was going on. We'd just brought home a new baby and now here we were, with an ambulance and a fire engine pulled up outside. At least six firemen came dashing into the house and I instantly felt more relaxed, and not just because I was now surrounded by handsome men in uniform! I could tell they meant business and were going to help me. They discussed putting me on a spinal board but, as they started tipping the board, my body rippled with pain and I yelped out. The firemen then decided that they would carry me downstairs, one step at a time, as rigidly as they could. It took three men to hold me straight and with each step a small shock went through me. The morphine had finally taken the edge off the pain, but I was far from comfortable. I will always be in debt to those firemen. Their professionalism at a time when I needed it most will never be forgotten.

I was put in the ambulance and hooked up to monitors as we began the eight-mile journey to Kings Mill Hospital, where Devon had been born just six days before. I was facing yet another stay in hospital, this time without my baby. I was distraught.

Chapter Ten

When we arrived at the hospital I felt very alone and scared. Graham was following on behind as he had to pack a bag for me and sort out Devon. By this time it was very late at night, but the A&E Department seemed really busy, with patients lying on beds all over the place. I wondered where Graham was and when I would get some answers as to why I was in so much pain. No one seemed at all concerned by my presence, and by now I was so dozy that I just didn't feel like fighting with anyone.

After a fitful, and excruciating, night, very early the next morning, we asked the nurses if I could be moved somewhere where I could have Devon with me, and where we would not have to stick to normal visiting hours so I could bond with my newborn. I was moved to a lovely private room with an en suite bathroom. I was on hourly observations at this point and had met a lovely student nurse called Bruce. He was a total charmer and really good at his job. He loved having a newborn on the ward and made a huge fuss of Devon whenever he popped in to conduct my checks. However, when he popped in for his final observation before lunch, he left the room immediately after taking my temperature. Within seconds the door had been flung open and several doctors and nurses came bounding into the room. When Bruce had taken my temperature it was 39.9 degrees – dangerously high. Each of the people around me wore a badge that said 'Critical Care Team', but I didn't feel ill at all. By now I was just really scared.

Once I was stable the doctor said that he wanted me to undergo a scan to see if they could finally diagnose the cause of my pain, spasms and increasing temperature. I was scared to death of them moving me because of the pain, but the nurse promised she would come with me and help them to move me into the scanner.

We left my little room shortly afterwards and made our way into the scan room, while Graham stood helplessly at the door. An MRI scan takes between 45 minutes and an hour to complete. If you so much as move a muscle they have to repeat elements of the scan, so you can imagine just how nerve-racking it was being wedged inside a larger version of a Smarties tube while my body was still in spasms. The noises inside an MRI scanner are also extremely off-putting. The magnets within the scanner rub together and sound like a pneumatic drill and, although you're given a set of headphones, the noise is so loud that you can seldom hear anything else. This was first time I'd ever been inside a 'Smarties tube' within a scanner before and I was terrified.

Soon enough the scan was over and I was taken back to the ward, but shortly afterwards the doctor came back into the room and told me I'd need yet another scan. The first MRI had revealed that I had the beginnings of MRSA growing in my body, which had probably been contracted following my C-section, and they were keen to have a better look at where the infection was.

That evening Graham's dad popped in to see me. We had asked him to look after Devon for the night so that Graham could stay with me. Graham's dad was an angel and agreed instantly, even though he was in his 70s and it had been a long time since he'd last cradled a newborn. I knew we could completely trust him, and was just happy to have Graham with me. While he was with us the doctor came in with two assistants. They asked me if it was okay to discuss my diagnosis in front of Howard, Graham's dad. I agreed; I had very few secrets any more!

The doctor addressed me with pity in his eyes, and explained that my cancer had returned. It had spread to my bones, leaving them so weak that my back was fractured in three places. I also had a tumour the size of an egg in my sacrum, which is at the base of the spine, as well as shadowing in that area.

It took a moment for the news to sink in, although when it did I simply went into autopilot. I remember thinking, 'Right then, that's more chemo!' I was adamant that I'd fight even harder this time. I had to, for Devon.

That night I lay in bed and prayed that everything would be okay.

Chapter Eleven

My MRSA infection meant that I was prescribed three bags of IV antibiotics each day for two weeks to help me to get better. Those two weeks dragged by and I started to become really angry at not being able to bond properly with my son. I remember waking up one day and turning the television on to see *This Morning* while I waited for Graham and Devon to arrive. Their guest was a lady who had lost her baby and it suddenly hit me, like that proverbial tonne of bricks, how lucky we were. As long as our baby was fit and healthy, nothing else mattered. I felt as though I had been given a wake-up call, and insisted on feeding and changing Devon at every opportunity when they eventually arrived.

Equally, I knew how hard things were for Graham, but I had every faith in his abilities. He had proved himself time and time again, under circumstances that even the most experienced father would have struggled with, and I was, and still am, incredibly proud of him.

* * *

Naomi Thomas

The weeks progressed and nothing more had been said about my cancer. My parents had come to visit me and see Devon for the first time, and I even had two old school friends pop in to say hello. Their support meant a great deal to us; this was meant to be such a special time, but so far Devon had spent more time in hospital with me than in his own home.

By day 12 I'd had enough. When the pharmacist came round to take a look at my drug chart I asked her to prepare my tablets for going home.

'Are you being discharged today? You must be so relieved!' The pharmacist looked pleased for me.

'No, I'm discharging myself.'

A few minutes later my doctor walked into the room with a bag of antibiotics. She smiled.

'How about making this your last one? You don't want to be here any longer, do you?' The relief was immense. I just wanted to get home. The pain in my back was finally under control thanks to a huge concoction of drugs. I still couldn't walk unaided but, as I hobbled out to the car, I listened to the birds singing and gazed up at the blue sky, feeling lucky to be alive.

The next step was an appointment with oncologist Dr Khan to discuss the rest of my treatment. During my last bout I had decided to do everything but chemo again; my hair had just about reached a nice length and looked like a deliberate style again. I didn't know if I was strong enough for round two. In no time at all the appointment day arrived. I didn't beat about the bush and asked Dr Khan straight away what my new diagnosis meant.

'Do you really want to know?' she asked quietly. I did, although the fear was rising inside me. Graham squeezed my hand.

'This type of cancer is incurable. We can treat it, but not cure it, and one day it will take your life. I'm afraid you won't live a long and healthy life.' Graham and I looked at each other and both burst into tears. The nurse and Dr Khan looked visibly emotional too. We were so unprepared for this diagnosis – all this time I had thought it would be another fight that I could win.

Despite my initial reservations it was decided that I would have chemotherapy again, as well as a possible operation at the Queen's Medical Centre in Nottingham. They had a specialist spinal department, which would be able to cope with the demands of such a complex procedure. I remember walking out into the car park and bursting into tears again. Graham hugged me tightly and, by the time I was in the car ready to go home, I had decided that I was going to put everything into winning this fight, because I had a son who needed me and nothing could take me away from him.

* * *

Not long after that fateful appointment we went to see the spinal surgeon to discuss my options. I could either have my unstable pelvis and spine cemented and screwed in place, or a much more complicated operation to try and remove and reconstruct as much as possible. The first option carried the risk that nothing further could be done should the procedure not work or my bones degenerate further, while the second would mean severing the nerve that controlled my right leg, leaving me unable to walk or drive unaided. It was a difficult, upsetting decision, but I eventually opted for the spinal surgery. Disabled or not, it seemed the best option, and, while we'd done enough research to know that taking the cancer away wouldn't cure me, it would hopefully provide the best long-term result.

The operation was to take over eight hours and would leave me off my feet for many weeks. My next huge decision was when to opt for the surgery; did I go straight for it to prevent any further damage to my spine, or wait until the chemotherapy had finished? We agonised for so long, but eventually decided to go for the operation once the chemo-therapy had finished. So here I was facing yet another six months of chemotherapy. How would I manage this time with a newborn baby and being so far away from family and friends?

* * *

No Ordinary Wedding Planner

One thing was certain: our wedding would have to be put on hold yet again. This time we made the difficult decision to cancel it completely, unsure if we'd ever be able to afford it, or if I'd be well enough to walk down the aisle. I couldn't bear the thought of hobbling towards my groom on crutches. We toyed with the idea of rushing to a registry office, but we could barely afford the registrar's fees, and had wanted a bigger celebration with friends and family. I also wanted a day that Devon could share in, as it's unlikely that I will live to see his wedding. Being a wedding planner, I was afraid there would be a lot of pressure on us to have the biggest and best day ever. There was nothing else for it; the wedding would have to wait, indefinitely.

We had decided to plan a family holiday for the following year. It was now late October and my treatment would finish in May. Graham and I asked our families to contribute money as a Christmas present, in the hopes that we could afford one last getaway before I was faced with a lifetime of disability. Our families did all that they could and gave us so much, with spending money left over. We were truly touched.

The chemotherapy was much tougher this time round, hitting my body straight away and sapping my white blood cells. Any bugs that were going around were an instant danger; a common cold could be fatal to someone with a blood count as low as mine. Each time I had a session of chemotherapy I got ill, ending up in hospital for short stays every now and again. Luckily, though, this round of treatment was much more infrequent than my last, occurring just once every three weeks for six sessions.

Shortly before Valentine's Day I was admitted to hospital with a temperature and a throat that seared with pain. The following Monday morning I was seen by a specialist. A swift look confirmed that I had laryngitis and yet more days in hospital were prescribed. I was finally allowed to go home on Valentine's Day, and Graham and I enjoyed a snuggle on the sofa. Such a small gesture, but being away from each other so much was simply serving to make us even stronger.

As I began the steady slope towards the end of chemotherapy, I didn't feel any of the relief that I'd experienced before. There was just an ever-growing sense of dread that the worst was yet to come.

Chapter Twelve

As planned, we booked a holiday for the three of us to Tenerife at the beginning of May. We were due to fly out a week or so after my final chemotherapy session, cramming it in before the operation. When we arrived in Tenerife I felt ever so slightly off, and could really feel the cold. I also struggled to walk any distance at all, and ended up spending my week sitting by the pool in my towel while the boys had great fun splashing around. It all sounds rather miserable, but looking back we had a superb time; it was just what we needed after the horrendous couple of years that we'd had.

In Tenerife it was as though my cancer didn't exist, and nothing and no one could touch us. As the plane's wheels hit the tarmac, though, everything flooded back. I was days away from a life-changing operation; this was something that I wasn't just going to bounce back from. I spent so many hours thinking about the operation, the pain I could be in, the long recovery period and the very real chance of being left disabled afterwards. Would I even be able to hold Devon and stand up? Little things like driving myself suddenly seemed so important now that I faced losing them for ever.

I went to see the surgeon two days prior to the operation. He explained that he'd conducted a lot of research following our last visit, and having spoken to other surgeons from across the world it transpired that the operation would be much longer than first thought, with a far greater recovery time and an extended hospital stay. Everyone he had spoken to would be reluctant to carry out the operation owing to the massive risks involved; it seemed that the positive outcome was outweighed significantly by the potential complications and side effects. The surgeon said that, despite his reservations, he would still go ahead with the operation if it was what I really wanted. However, only part of the tumour could be removed, little altering my prognosis, and the negative implications of the surgery would leave me with yet more to contend with. I decided not to go ahead with the operation and, to this day, I know I made the right choice.

I was started on a course of Herceptin and Tamoxifen, which were designed to remove the hormones that feed my type of cancer. Herceptin was to be administered via three-weekly intravenous drips that would hopefully keep me stable, and alive, for as long as possible.

Within a few short weeks I was back at the hospital for yet more scans to assess the cancer's response to the chemotherapy, and to see if my bones were any stronger. I knew that if they weren't I still had the option of having my pelvis cemented, which was a much more straightforward procedure.

During the scan a small amount of dye was injected into my veins. As the machine finished whirling and whizzing above me, I began to feel a weird sensation in my right eye. On my way back to the changing room I caught sight of myself in a mirror. I stared in shock – my eye was heavily swollen. I soon found myself in A&E, where it emerged I was having an allergic reaction to the dye that had been used during my scan. I was given an antihistamine injection to try and stem the swelling, but my eye didn't show any signs of returning to normal. I was sent home with daily steroids in the hopes that it would right itself over time.

Over the next few days I began to feel more and more low. I remember sitting on the lounge floor one morning and just sobbing, all the while having no idea what I was crying about; I just knew that the harder I tried to stop, the more I wanted to cry. I had never felt that low before and it was starting to really scare me. To top it all off Graham had contracted a sickness bug and, what with me constantly crying and him rushing to the loo every five minutes, we were really struggling with Devon. Finally, Graham called my parents and they agreed to come and stay with us for a few days.

Within a few days of my scan, Graham started to wonder if the steroids were interfering with my other medications. A quick call to the doctors confirmed Graham's suspicions and I was advised to stop taking the tablets immediately. Luckily I felt better within hours of coming off the steroids; the crying stopped and, incidentally, so did Graham's sickness. Nevertheless, it had dawned on us just how far from our friends and family we were, and how stuck we'd be if something really serious happened. My parents agreed, and offered us their full support if we chose to move back to the West Country.

Although I was in no hurry to return, I knew that Graham had been finding it increasingly difficult not knowing anyone or having any help with caring for Devon and me. He didn't have anywhere he could just go to let off steam and he was desperately missing his friends and being by the sea. Although my cancer was still there and always would be now, my active treatment had come to an end and I just wanted to return to some semblance of normality – whatever 'normality' was! After a lot of thinking,

I agreed to the move on one condition – that Graham did all the house hunting. His challenge was set!

Chapter Thirteen

As usual, Graham landed on his feet and managed to find us a stunning house almost immediately, but with us being 250 miles away it really wasn't feasible to go and visit the house, especially as we already had a trip to Cornwall scheduled; that journey was just too expensive to make twice! We also couldn't wait until we visited Cornwall before we viewed the property; it was gorgeous, and would no doubt have been taken off the market by then. The notice on our house in Nottingham had to be handed in as soon as possible, so we asked my dad to view the new place for us. He was happy to, and we briefed him on everything we wanted to know before agreeing to take the house on. I also made him promise that he would take hundreds of photos.

The viewing was arranged for the very next day and I was bursting to hear how my dad had got on. He thought the house would be perfect for us, although he admitted that he had taken barely any photos. He explained that all the fixtures, fittings and décor were modern, though, and that we wouldn't be disappointed.

We decided that we would go for it, signing a six-month let initially. I was absolutely terrified, never having been so spontaneous when it came to houses before. The short let did mean that we would be able to move fairly quickly if it all went wrong, but I was so keen for it to be right – to find home. I was looking forward to spending time with my boys and, with the property being in a rural location, having lots of welly walks and perhaps even growing our own vegetables.

A couple of weeks later we set off on our trip to Cornwall. We had asked the estate agent if we could view the house on our way down, but had been told that the present tenant was moving out that day so it wouldn't be possible. We were due to move just one week later and made the decision that, if the tenant had gone by the time we were making our way home, we would peek through the windows.

Pulling up on to the driveway, we noticed a builder's van parked outside and hoped that we could persuade him to let us look around. Trotting round to the side of the house, we found the builder working and quickly explained who we were. He was a really likeable chap and, with a glint in his eye, said, 'Mmm, I'm sure I could show you around. Specially as I'm the landlord!' Graham and I couldn't believe our luck. Our new landlord, Mark, gave us a little tour of the house and it blew us away, wildly exceeded all of our expectations. On top of it all there was a downstairs bathroom with a little room next door, which could be used as a bedroom, as well as disabled access throughout – perfect for when my back flared up and I was unable to use the stairs. We headed back to Nottingham filled with excitement at what the future had in store for us.

We soon settled into our new home, and within a couple of days the house looked as though we had lived there for ever. One afternoon I was exploring the local supermarket when I saw a poster advertising the Macmillan campaign for a Girls Night In. I began to think that I should try and organise something to celebrate the fact that I was back where I belonged, as well as raising a few pounds for the charities that had helped me over the past couple of years.

I put some feelers out and within a few days the event had grown so big that there was no way I could hold it at my home. A few calls to find some raffle prizes had soon turned my spare room into a treasure trove of wonderful gifts, and the guest list was now creeping up. I decided to move the event to a local house in Sidmouth, which was absolutely perfect for all sorts of occasions; in fact we'd held Devon's christening there earlier that year. It also had a personal connection, as my dad had been born in the cellar when my nan and granddad had lived there.

I approached the local paper, the *Sidmouth Herald*, and explained my plans and reasons behind hosting the event. Soon the story was plastered all over the front page, as well as featuring in the paper every week afterwards, and my phone was ringing with offers of help and raffle prizes. We decided to call the event 'Pink Ladies Day', and to offer women of all ages the chance to pop along and be pampered for the evening. We would have cocktails, hair stylists, make-up lessons, spray tanning, nail art and pedicures, Reiki, scarves to buy, a photographer, and more – you name it and we had thought of it! Local personality Judy Spiers had been invited along to officially open the event, and Olympic silver medallist Mary King had agreed to draw the raffle.

It wasn't long before the national press cottoned on to my story. I'll never forget the day the *Sun* called me to do an interview! It helped that I was so passionate about the cause; all I wanted to do was raise awareness of the instances of breast cancer in younger people and decided that I would do anything that I could to educate people about it.

The event was planned for 15 January 2012 and there was a real buzz in the air. Wherever I went I was stopped by strangers who seemed to know my name. Just before Christmas I received a call from the local paper saying that a local lady, Sam Williams, had been in contact and really wanted to help. I got in touch with her straight away and we arranged to meet.

Meeting Sam was a wonderful experience; we chatted for hours as though we'd known each other for years. Sam had a background in event organising, and was just starting her own wedding planning business in Devon. She wanted to help as much as possible with the Pink Ladies Day and she was the sort of person I needed in my life; a real doer who wanted to get on with things. Within hours Sam had brought so much to the table. She was hugely organised and almost doubled our support network. She and her daughter were soon delivering, and she worked tirelessly to attract stallholders and raffle prizes. I will be forever grateful for her support.

Around this time our special friends Dave and Sophie got engaged in Paris. They soon approached me and asked for some assistance with finding their wedding venue. They wanted to get married in Somerset the following September and, while I didn't know the area very well yet, I wasn't fazed by the challenge. I quickly arranged viewings of venues across the county, but nothing seemed to really hit the nail on the head. Dave and Sophie were just about to book a venue close to Bath, simply because they wanted to get something sorted. I told them to hold off, desperate that they shouldn't settle for second best.

It wasn't long before I came across an amazing venue nearby: St Audries Park. The house looked absolutely stunning. It was going to be outside of their budget, surely? However, one look at their 'Special Offers' page suggested otherwise, and I decided to go and have a look at it the very next day.

St Audries Park was just 35 minutes away from where we all lived, on the edge of the countryside towards the coast. As I made my way down the long sweeping driveway the house suddenly came into view and my heart skipped a beat. From the outside it looked absolutely perfect, although I knew it was far too soon to pass any judgement on the venue. I've lost count of the times I have seen and loved a venue, only to find that their carpet clashes with their walls, or that the décor makes it impossible to have a colour scheme of your own.

However, St Audries Park did not disappoint. The place was incredible, with plenty of rooms including a separate room for dancing, and one for a wedding breakfast. The staff were lovely and went out of their way to make you feel special. Lynn, who showed me around, took me across the beautifully manicured gardens to the Orangery, where ceremonies took place. The Orangery was a white and glass building with grey flagstone flooring, a cream aisle runner, ivy-twined pillars, and music playing from carefully placed speakers. The room completely took my breath away. In all my years of wedding planning, I had never before been rendered speechless by a venue.

Lynn turned to me and smiled. She asked me if I was blown away. Not a word would come out of my mouth; I could only nod. St Audries Park was the perfect venue for Dave and Sophie and so I called them straight away and arranged for them to visit after work that day.

Later that evening Dave called. The couple was so excited and had absolutely loved St Audries, booking it there and then. I was so pleased for them, but felt insanely jealous at the same time. I was desperate to get married at the venue too and, despite their amazing deals, knew that we could never afford it. All of our savings had gone towards getting us through the last two years and I knew I had to come to terms with the fact that I might never marry Graham. That night, I am embarrassed to say, I sobbed my heart out. There it was, the venue of my dreams, and it was someone else getting married there. I cried like a spoiled girl, but it hurt so much.

Chapter Fourteen

One day while I was working with Sam, she suddenly turned to me and announced, 'I want to help you to get married for as little money as possible.' I was stunned; we still barely knew each other. Sam had seen just how generous people could be during the run up to Pink Ladies Day and she was certain that we could get the same amount of support for our wedding. Graham and I were overwhelmed by Sam's generosity and couldn't thank her enough. She was soon hard at work and had offers flooding in from every direction.

I paid a visit to the bridal boutique where I'd tried on my very first dress in the days after we became engaged, and was amazed to be offered the gorgeous Maggie Sottero gown for just cost price. A quick call to the supplier in America confirmed that they had one in my size. I felt so fortunate. Unfortunately I wasn't able to order the dress that day as there was still one thing dictating the possibility of a wedding. Sam loved St Audries Park too, but it was still going to be pretty impossible for us to get together the funds to pay for the venue.

The local newspaper was closely covering the story of our wedding as events unfolded and we were getting many messages of encouragement from across the town. One day a reporter from the paper called to say that there was a lady who wanted to get in touch with me. She called to say that she was desperate to help Graham and me marry, and wanted to donate £500 towards the wedding. I was over-whelmed that a stranger could do anything so unbe-lievably kind. She didn't know my family or me, and although she had a holiday home in Sidmouth she actually lived miles away. She didn't want any recog-nition for the donation, but said if I wanted to mention it at all to call her 'Mary Poppins'. So that was that; Mary Poppins had got the ball well and truly rolling, and helped me to believe that perhaps our dreams could come true after all.

One afternoon on Facebook I came across a charity called the Karen Trust, which had been set up by a man called Joe who had lost his sister Karen to cancer. Their motto was to count the memories, not the years, and they organised special things for people who wanted to make those memories while they still could. I felt that I had nothing to lose, and decided to get in contact to see if they could help with the cost of our wedding. I spoke to a lovely

Irish lady called Mary. She immediately put me at ease, listening to my story and promising to get back to me as soon as she had spoken with the board.

A few days later Graham and I were in the garage while our car was having its MOT when Mary rang me back. She told me that the Karen Trust wanted to help and would donate over half of the money required for our venue. I started to cry; yet again people were being so lovely to us when they didn't even know us.

A family member had offered to buy my dress for me, although I knew it was unlikely that the one I really wanted would still be available. With that in mind I went off to look for an alternative, but in the meantime Sam had called the original dress shop to enquire about the Maggie Sottero gown on the off-chance that it would still be available. Later that day she called me.

'Good news! The owner of the shop was so touched by your story that she bought the dress in the hopes that you'd be back in. She's got it there waiting for you.' I couldn't believe it. Our wedding day was becoming the event of fairy tales.

While all of this had been going on we were also putting the finishing touches to Pink Ladies Day. The press were booked to come and cover it, and everyone was so excited. When the day finally arrived I felt an overwhelming sense of relief. I had put so much of my heart and soul into the event that I was just glad we'd pulled it off. I was also desperate for it to be a success so that we could raise as much money as possible for the three charities that had helped me since my diagnosis.

As we opened the doors of the venue at 2pm there were already people waiting outside and making their way down the long driveway towards the grand house. I stood next to Sam, gazing at all of the guests, and felt so proud of what we'd achieved. As the press looked on Judy Spiers cut the ribbon and officially opened the Pink Ladies Day; I couldn't have been prouder. Devon came to the ladies day with me, and I hope that one day he will look back at the photos and be proud of my achievements too.

There was soon a real buzz emanating from within Kennaway House. Each room was filled with people having a good time, while a gospel choir sang in the entrance hall, and a photographer snapped pictures of those who'd been treated to a makeover. More and more people were arriving, and many came over to tell me how I was their inspiration. I had also noticed several guests popping folded notes into the collection tins, and many people had turned up bearing gifts of all shapes and sizes for me.

Shortly before the raffle was due to be drawn I broke down in the corridor. I was so overwhelmed by the love and support surrounding me. In just over four hours the Pink Ladies Day had greeted 400 people and raised nearly £4,500. It exceeded every expectation. Even my old school tutor had turned up to support me. As I stood at the front of the room to announce the raffle draw I felt all eyes on me; this was my moment to thank everyone who had made the day possible, but I broke down again and sobbed my way through the whole thing! I knew that my emotions had been significantly heightened due to my illness and medication, but I was also so touched by how the community had come together to support the charities closest to my heart.

Once the hype of the Pink Ladies Day had died down, I decided that I really wanted to start my own charity and help people. Suddenly it came to me; if I was so desperate to marry the love of my life before it was too late, then surely there must be others out there in a similar position. I'd seen so many young people in the hospitals when I'd been in for treatment and I knew that cancer, among many other terrible illnesses, was not restricted to the elderly.

I discussed the idea with Sam and Graham, and they both agreed that it sounded great. I threw some possible names on the table, desperate to give my charity an identity from the start, and decided upon The Wedding Wishing Well Foundation; after all, I would be helping couples' dreams to come true. I also made an appointment to go and see someone at my local voluntary service, hoping to gather some information and advice on starting a charity. Luckily the ladies at the voluntary service were a huge help and pointed me in the right direction. In no time at all The Wedding Wishing Well Foundation was born.

Chapter Fifteen

I got stuck straight into my new charity, approaching a number of different wedding-related businesses to see if, and how, they could help. Everyone I spoke to seemed to love the idea and I'd soon gathered a small database of companies that I could call upon when we had a wedding to organise.

I had decided that I didn't just want to operate my charity locally; I wanted The Wedding Wishing Well Foundation to help couples across the country. I had done my research and knew that there were no other organisations within the UK that were doing what I was proposing. I had big plans of the Foundation becoming a household name; in fact, the one and only name that people would think of when they came across a couple in need. I had also made the decision to try and build up the charity's database before taking on any weddings. I wanted to be able to approach each couple's special day with confidence, safe in the knowledge that we had plenty of help to call upon, no matter where the bride and groom were getting married. For that reason I chose not to publicise The Wedding Wishing Well Foundation beyond our tentative searches for help; the application form was on the website should anyone wish to apply, but I felt better knowing that we would be truly ready whenever we opened for business properly.

It was a few weeks before our wedding day, and I had been talked into having a hen night. While I was once the first person to head out on to the dance floor, clubbing really wasn't my thing any more so I suggested that a few friends come to mine for some food and drink, and to have a bit of pampering. Sam and my friend Shari instructed me to head out for the day, making me promise that I wouldn't return before mid-afternoon. Puzzled, I spent the morning doing some shopping and working out at the gym, all the while a little nervous about what would be waiting for me when I got home! When we pulled on to our driveway later on that day, we found that the front door had been attacked with banners and balloons. Graham and I went tentatively into the house, not knowing what we would find. As we made our way along the hall there were sticky notes all over the walls telling us to follow them, which we duly did. The second to last, stuck on the kitchen door, said, 'Guess what?!', while the next exclaimed, 'You're going to Egypt!' I looked up to see Shari videoing our reactions, the kitchen festooned with photos of Egyptian pyramids and camels. There was even a Cleopatra outfit hanging on the curtain rail, ready for me to put on. Graham and I both rushed over to the devious pair and gave them a massive hug each. It turned out that Sam had secretly arranged for a charity to donate a holiday for us. We'd had no idea, even when she'd started quizzing us about our dream holiday destination! The hotel looked incredible, and I can honestly say that it was one of the best moments of my life so far; Graham and I will always be indebted to Sam for what she has done for us.

The morning of our wedding finally arrived, and we were beyond excited as to what the day would bring. The evening before I had stayed in a cottage at the venue with my mum, bridesmaid Shari, and Sam, and we'd had a lovely evening together. I'd wanted Sam to be a part of it all, partly as a thank you for all she'd done, and because she'd become such a wonderful friend. As we got back to the cottage after going for a delicious meal together, the ladies presented me with a special gift from Graham. Apparently he'd been really nervous, unsure as to whether I'd like it, but he needn't have worried. Inside the carefully wrapped box was a book, which was filled with captions such as, 'When I first saw you I felt …' and 'Marrying you will be …', and he had decorated each page with photos of me, him and

Devon. It was so lovely that I burst into tears. This was yet another reminder of how lucky I was to have found my Prince Charming.

Before I began to get ready for the wedding I headed to a little church that was located within the grounds of St Audries. Since the grounds were so huge, the church was actually quite a distance from the main house. Graham and I had opted for a civil ceremony in the beautiful surroundings of the Orangery, rather than a full church service. Although I am not a regular churchgoer I do have a strong belief and class myself as a Christian. Graham is the total opposite, so it made sense for me to compromise and head to the church by myself before the day got under way. Quickly getting Devon and myself dressed, I crept across the grounds and into the back of the church to join the service, which had already begun. It's a tiny village church and was occupied by no more than ten people. Each one of them turned around and smiled as Devon and I entered; we were made to feel so welcome. The service was lovely and, afterwards, the vicar approached me to introduce herself. I explained that I was getting married at St Audries that day, as well as telling her about my illness. The vicar asked if she could pray for us at the altar. I always find that churches really bring out my emotions, and before long I had begun to cry. Once again I was touched by the kindness of strangers, as well as being overwhelmed by my wedding day and the circumstances surrounding it. I left the church after 20 minutes of peaceful quiet time and wandered back to the cottage where breakfast was waiting for us. Before long it was time for us to make our way to the main hall for the makeover to begin!

The morning of our wedding was a busy one, and people seemed to be scurrying here, there and everywhere doing jobs of all kinds. Devon was with me, being his usual boisterous self, so it took me much longer to get ready than I'd anticipated. Shari and her little boy, Archie, were with me all morning too and, despite the air being filled with excitement, I can remember feeling an overwhelming sense of calm. All I could think about was marrying the love of my life; nothing had ever felt so right before. Shortly before 2pm I got into my dream gown and Sam laced it up for me. There was just enough time to present Sam and Shari with their gifts, and for a few more tears, and I was ready to go. By 2.15pm (late, of course!) I was heading towards the Orangery, gingerly making my way down the corridors and stairs shielded by umbrellas so that no one caught a glimpse of my dress until I was walking down the aisle. As I approached I could hear a beautiful string quartet playing; this was it. My dad and I stood just inside the Orangery as Shari and Devon made their way down the aisle together, my son holding the rings on a cushion which he decided to throw onto the floor as soon as he knew people were looking. As my bridesmaid and little boy reached the end of their walk, with all eyes on them, Dad and I got into position.

My dad and I are very close and, while we don't have a tactile sort of relationship, I know that my dad loves me with all his heart and he is similarly aware of how much I love him. They do say that you usually marry a man very much like your father, and Graham is similar to my dad in a lot of ways. Being given away by my dad meant the world to me, and as we began to walk I could sense just how proud he was to be there, as well as being happy to pass me into the capable hands of Graham! I could now feel everyone looking at me, and glimpsed so many happy, as well as tearful, faces as I made my way towards my husband-to-be. I had so far managed to hold everything together, even though I was very conscious that I was late; I just wanted to run the rest of the way to be with Graham. His best man, Ben, gave him the nod and Graham turned around. As soon as he saw me he started to falter a little and he licked his lip – a sure sign of emotion bubbling to the surface! At this point I looked up to the sky and said a little prayer, thanking God that I was still alive and finally marrying the man of my dreams. I felt so lucky that I could literally have burst. Thankfully I had thought ahead, stuffing a tissue down the top of my dress before we'd left the room; when we finally made it to the front of the Orangery, it was soon out for a quick dab of my eyes!

We had chosen three very special people: my aunty Sue, Devon's godmother Chris, and our friend Zulieka, to do some readings for us. They all read with such clarity and emotion that it was all I could manage not to burst into tears again. Graham and I had written our own vows, neither knowing what the other was about to say. As we spoke I know we truly meant every single word. We managed a few peeks at our guests and could both see how moved they were too; I'd even spotted a few men wiping away the tears! When we were finally pronounced husband and wife the room erupted into cheers and applause. We had made it, against all odds, and were now married – as well as being a united front of Mummy and Daddy. Although cancer was still very much a part of our lives, we felt like the luckiest people in the whole world to have what we had.

As Graham and I left the Orangery we had a few moments to ourselves before heading out to greet our guests, who were waiting with confetti poised. Once again a huge cheer broke out as we made our way through the dried petals to the drinks reception, which was held on the lawns of St Audries. The sun came out just long enough for us to have some wonderful photos taken as memories of our special day. In addition to the drink there was an ice-cream cart, tasty canapés, a caricature artist, and lawn games for the children, including an egg-and-spoon race, croquet and sack races. There was even a team of nannies to watch over the little ones so that we could enjoy ourselves without the worry; Sam had thought of everything. The cocktails were served on trays, with mini cream teas presented on slate. By now the string quartet had joined us in the garden and was playing modern music, such as Lady Gaga – I have never heard her songs played in such a way before!

It wasn't long before we were called in for the wedding breakfast, which was served in a gorgeous room bedecked with artificial flowers, birdcages and displays of gold peonies. Each place setting had a gold-coloured charger plate, a handmade pearl napkin ring, and either a lottery scratch card or chocolate favour. Children had colouring books and pencils too; being a wedding planner, I am often worried that the finished product won't meet my expectations, but Sam's efforts had completely floored them. Taking centre stage was the stunning four-tiered wedding cake, which was decorated with lace, brooches and pale pink roses to match my dress and bouquet. It was breathtaking.

Before we knew it, it was time for the speeches. Both Graham and I wanted to say a few words. I was desperate to publicly thank everybody who had come together to make our day so special, and to tell Sam how much we appreciated her love and generosity. Of course I blubbed my way through the whole thing – it's a wonder anyone heard any of it! Sam blew me a kiss from where she sat, and I was relieved that she'd heard how much she meant to us.

The revelries went on into the night, with a guitarist and singer who I'd met at a charity function playing some great acoustic numbers. This was followed by a disco and casino; great fun! Our first dance was our final official duty of the day, and we waltzed around the floor to an emotional Alicia Keys song, before taking things up a notch and dancing to Temper Trap. Devon had also joined us for a boogie by this point! By 10pm I was absolutely pooped. My dress was so heavy that it was causing a cramping sensation in my abdominal muscles, and I was severely flagging. I went up to our room to get changed, briefly returning to the party to say my goodnights. I think people were shocked to see me leaving so soon, but I knew that if I had pushed myself any harder I would regret it for weeks. I could hear the party continuing downstairs long after I'd made my way up to our room, but I didn't mind at all. In fact I was so pleased that everyone was enjoying themselves, and was just so happy to have married Graham.

Chapter Sixteen

Most brides soon plummet back to reality with a big bump after their wedding day, but not me; we still had so much to look forward to. An old school friend of Graham's had offered us some time in her log cabin on the outskirts of Exeter and, although it wasn't very far from home or the city, it was so rural that it felt a million miles from civilisation. With a gorgeous view over a fishing lake, as well as a hot tub, it was just what we needed to unwind.

It was Graham's birthday while we were staying in the log cabin and I had secretly arranged for my parents, Graham's mum and his grandma to come over for afternoon tea. They crept up to the door and rang the bell. Graham was very confused as to whom it might be, but was so chuffed to see his family there to share his special day. We spent his birthday enjoying the hot tub and drinking bubbly!

* * *

No Ordinary Wedding Planner

Our time at the log cabin soon passed and, after spending a few short days at home, we were jetting off for our week-long holiday in Egypt, which had been donated to us by a wonderful Exeter-based charity, Dream-a-Way. Waking up at the Sensatori Resort in Egypt the next morning was amazing. Opening our curtains was an adventure in itself; our room overlooked the ocean, and the view was magnificent. There were several swimming pools, including one especially for children with slides, and an infinity pool with jets; I was in heaven!

I celebrated my 30th birthday in Egypt and spent the day swimming with dolphins. Upon returning to the hotel room, we found that the staff had decorated the bed with towel sculptures, flower petals and a big cake, as well as all of the birthday cards that I had opened that morning from people at home. It was a birthday to remember, and the dolphins were yet another item ticked off my 'bucket list'!

In no time at all our week in Egypt was over and we were back to reality with a bump, with my treatment booked in the following day. I have to have three-weekly treatments of Herceptin and Zometa, which has essentially put my body into the menopause so that my cancer has no oestrogen to feed from, while also strengthening my bones. Luckily I am now able to have treatment at home, rather than making regular trips to the hospital, and I was sitting on the sofa with the needle embedded in my chest when Graham brought me the morning's post.

One envelope stood out. It was addressed to 'The Wedding Wishing Well Foundation'. As I opened the letter and pulled out the wedge of paper inside, I saw that it was one of our application forms. I started reading immediately. The letter had come from a lady called Emma, who had secondary breast cancer just like me. Her cancer had spread to her bones initially, but was now in her brain too. Her words hit a nerve with me immediately and I could feel tears in my eyes. I always take my own illness with a pinch of salt, but it made me so sad to hear that someone was suffering so much. I knew that this time would come for me too, but I hadn't been prepared for it at all.

Seconds later, I'd decided that I needed to help this couple to marry before it was too late, although I knew we'd have a tight budget as the charity was still in its infancy. Emma and her fiancé Steve were from Derbyshire and wanted to marry in an intimate ceremony at Caerlaverock Castle in Scotland, with a party for friends back in their home town a week later. This meant that certain items, such as wedding cakes, would need to be duplicated and it would take a lot of travelling just before Christmas. However, we had four months to plan and I was drawn to help this very special couple.

No Ordinary Wedding Planner

Within days I had contacted the couple and told them that The Wedding Wishing Well Foundation would help them. I got to work straight away and contacted the various venues, as well as ringing cake makers, photographers, pipers, hair and make-up artists, and other suppliers to see if they could (and would) donate their time for the couple. So many people said 'yes' that within those four months we were almost ready to go.

Graham had decided to come with me for this first wedding, making sure I had plenty of help with the driving and lugging around of heavy items! Although I was still capable of driving, lengthy car journeys take their toll quite quickly. Devon, of course, came too, and we hoped that we'd have the opportunity to see a little of Scotland while we were there. The drive up to Scotland was stunning in itself. There had been a fair bit of snow in the Lake District and, as we drove past, the mountains were absolutely covered; the scenery was incredible. Sights like that always make me feel lucky to be alive, as simple as that sounds.

I was nervous about the charity's first wedding but, with my previous wedding planning experience, knew that I was capable of pulling it off. I was just so desperate for the day to be the best of Emma and Steve's lives, just as mine and Graham's had been six months before. On the morning of the wedding I got ready and quickly dashed to the venue to make sure that Emma was there, and that her hair and make-up artists had arrived on time. It was good to see her excited, although she looked nervous too. I then went downstairs to oversee the delivery of the cake, decorations and flowers. Before long it was time for me to whizz off to the castle itself, helping to set everything up prior to the guests' arrival. Caerlaverock Castle, with its deep moat, is absolutely stunning from the front, although the back is now in ruins. That morning the wind was sweeping through the castle's walls, making it bitterly cold. I set up a few tea lights and little tots of whisky, which were sure to warm the guests, as well as some ginger for anyone who wanted some. We also had bubbles, rather than confetti, which were going to look beautiful.

Once everything was set up I made my way across the castle's bridge to greet the piper and wait for the bridal car. The groom arrived on time with the couple's dog, a little ribbon tied on his collar. As Emma's car finally pulled in, it dawned on me just how far The Wedding Wishing Well Foundation had come in 11 short months. Without the charity's help it was unlikely that Emma and Steve would have been able to marry at all, or at least on the scale that we had achieved; it really was a dream day. Emma, looking absolutely stunning, got out of the car and walked into the castle with her father by her side. As she made her way down the makeshift aisle tears prickled in my eyes; I couldn't help but be reminded of my own special day and what it had meant to Graham and me. As we'd not been able to find a videographer I filmed the ceremony myself with shaky hands – another skill to add to my CV!

As with all weddings, the day passed by in a blur. The next morning I made my way between the venues to pack everything away, as well as going to say 'goodbye' to the new Mr and Mrs Oakey. They were filled with thanks and praise for everything we'd achieved for them, although the fun wasn't over yet; we still had their party in Derbyshire to go.

Later that week I was on the move again, and travelled up to Derbyshire to set up a lovely reception for Emma and Steve at a local tourist attraction called Conkers. The venue's event planner, Joy, was absolutely amazing and helped me to set everything up and make the evening as special as she could. It's always lovely to meet people who share my passion.

Once again the revelries were soon over and it was time to say goodbye to Steve and Emma, which was so hard. We had been in daily contact for six months and now our involvement in their lives, and theirs in mine, was over. It was time to move on to the charity's next project. Thankfully many of our couples keep in touch beyond the wedding day, although, when working with people affected by terminal illness, the inevitable will happen and is not always far away.

Chapter Seventeen

Just before Christmas I received a phone call from the editor of *Wedding Ideas* magazine. She told me that I had been nominated for their Bride of the Year Award, and that I was one of the finalists. I couldn't quite believe what I was hearing! As the phone had rung, I'd just been about to whizz out of the door and go to the local garden centre. However, I was now being asked to pop in to see the staff of the magazine and, as their offices were just six miles away from our home, I agreed to visit them as we drove past.

Arriving at the *Wedding Ideas* magazine offices, it occurred to me that we should have got changed before leaping into the car; waiting for us was a camera, which was ready to film a short video that would be shown on the evening of the awards. We both felt a little silly in our gardening clothes, but the staff members were so friendly and welcoming that we put our fears to one side and chatted about The Wedding Wishing Well Foundation, my health, and Graham's feelings about what I do.

After the interview Rachel, the magazine's editor, told us that the awards ceremony would be held after Christmas at the Tower Hotel in London. This was going to be my first time attending an event of this magnitude and I was so excited. Rachel revealed that I had been nominated by many of the suppliers who had put our wedding together. It was lovely to know that all of those people had taken the time to vote for me, and I was yet again pleasantly surprised by the warmth of relative strangers.

The Wedding Ideas Awards is an annual event that honours a number of bridal categories, including dress designer, photographer, venue, and more. Even if I didn't win, the evening would be a fantastic opportunity for networking and meeting new contacts. It was an enormous privilege just to have been nominated. Rachel ended our meeting by saying that she'd arrange for me to try on a few dresses by designers that were connected with the magazine, as well as organising for me to have my hair and make-up done on the evening. This was going to be an amazing evening – I could just feel it.

Later that week I received another phone call, this time to say that I'd been nominated for the Real People and Mecca Bingo Community Champions Award for their Caring Person category. I was told that I'd won that particular category and that I'd need to go to London for the overall awards ceremony, where all finalists were to be gathered to decide upon an eventual winner. Winning the Caring Person category meant that I would automatically receive a prize of £1,000, which was going to be a huge help to the charity. It turned out that both awards ceremonies were within days of each other, so Graham and I decided to book a hotel in London for the long weekend.

The night of the Wedding Ideas Awards arrived and we made our way into the reception of the Tower Hotel. Tower Bridge was illuminated and it looked incredible. Graham and I were soon caught up in lots of hustle and bustle outside. We were worried at first that we were in the wrong place, but soon came to realise that the flashing bulbs of photographers' cameras were for us! As we sashayed down the red carpet with other guests we felt like real celebrities, with the 'paparazzi' shouting for our attention.

Once we got inside the room was absolutely electric, with magicians, Vodka luges and photographers everywhere. I'd had my hair and make-up done and felt a million dollars, while Graham looked as gorgeous as ever in his tuxedo. After a short while we were called to dinner, entering the biggest room I'd ever seen, which was filled with over 300 people. There was a massive stage, with a huge screen and moody pink lighting to match the flowers, chair covers and sashes; I knew this was where the prizes would be awarded, and the nerves kicked in a little.

No Ordinary Wedding Planner

Following a delicious meal the awards ceremony soon began. I knew that the last award would be the Bride of the Year, and glanced around the room trying to fathom who I was up against. The prizes started rolling out; St Audries Park won best venue, while Maggie Sottero won the award for bridal wear. The other awards whizzed past, until it was time for the Bride of the Year. Rachel stepped up to the microphone and began to talk about the award, outlining the qualities of the winning bride. For a moment I was convinced it sounded like she was talking about me, but it wasn't until our video (complete with gardening clobber) flashed up on the big screen that I knew for sure. I'd won. I was absolutely gobsmacked and felt Graham squeezing my hand tightly. Finally my name was called, and it flashed up on the screen in giant letters. Shaking, I made my way to the stage, helped up the steps by the toastmaster. Rachel gave me a huge hug and kiss, and I was given a bunch of flowers and the award.

It was a huge moment for me. Thankfully I'd prepared a speech on the off chance, which had been shoved in my bag so that I wouldn't fumble my words and waste the opportunity. For the first time in my life I managed to hold everything together and speak to a room full of people, never once letting my voice falter. As I peeped over my bit of paper I could see men and women in the audience crying, although the room was so quiet and still that you could have heard a pin drop. I finished my speech by dedicating the award to Devon; he was, and still is, my reason for breathing and the very inspiration behind my fight.

I returned to my seat to a standing ovation and a round of applause. As the awards came to an end I felt a tap on my shoulder. The owner of a bridal wear shop introduced himself, handing me his business card and saying that he wanted to help The Wedding Wishing Well Foundation in any way possible. I sat open-mouthed for a few moments until I felt another tap, again someone wanting to help. This carried on for about 20 minutes as people literally queued up on either side of me, waiting their turn to offer assistance. I got some truly amazing offers that evening. Of course, some ended in nothing, but many have become fantastic supporters of the charity, including Maggie Sottero. To have such a renowned manufacturer on board has been truly wonderful.

As the charity grew, I knew it was time to move out of my home office and into somewhere where I could really focus on The Wedding Wishing Well Foundation. As soon as we got back to Somerset I began to search for a new office. Within a few weeks, and with a lot of blood, sweat and tears (mainly from Graham), I moved into the new premises, and finally the charity could breathe and grow. The emails started coming in at a huge rate of knots, and the phone was ringing constantly. The Wedding Wishing Well Foundation was about to become bigger than I ever could have envisaged.

Chapter Eighteen

Although small donations had been coming in over the last few months, it was time to hold a fundraiser that would bring in a more significant amount; enough to cover a wedding, perhaps! It was also time we celebrated the work that some of our volunteers had achieved over the last year or so, as well as taking the opportunity to launch the charity officially. A Masquerade Ball seemed like the perfect way to do all of these.

The Wedding Wishing Well Foundation was lucky enough to be given the use of a beautiful venue, Somerset Woodlands Castle, in which to hold the ball, while the catering was offered to us for a reduced fee. We were also given some fabulous decorations and, in no time at all, the evening of the ball was upon us. We had an absolutely brilliant night, including entertainment provided by the Singing Waiters, who went down a storm! The best part of the night, though, was the outstanding total of £3,234, which was raised by those in attendance.

The Masquerade Ball had also gone a long way towards raising our profile in the local area; no one could say they hadn't heard of us after that! We gave out two awards that evening – the Volunteer of the Year Award, and the Going the Extra Mile Award, which were presented to two deserving volunteers. It was lovely to be able to give my team the recognition that they deserved.

In March we were approached by an agency in Birmingham that was helping a gentleman who had been given very little time left to live. He was desperate to marry his girlfriend and we quickly agreed to help him, even though we had just eight days in which to pull it all together. This would be our greatest race against time yet, but I was determined that we'd make it happen. In just six days we'd organised everything we needed; I was so proud that we'd achieved the seemingly impossible. The doctors were really concerned that Stephen, the groom, wouldn't live to see his wedding, but, against all odds, he made it, and he and his bride Chris enjoyed their dream day. Even though our weddings are essentially for the couple, the day has a real impact on their family and friends too. It is perhaps the first time for a long time, and maybe even the last time, that they see their loved one smile, and it means so much that we can be a part of making these memories. These are special moments that the couple and their family can hold on to, even in their darkest days. Marriage is something that can never be taken away from them.

Before my diagnosis I'd have laughed at you if you had said I would soon be standing up in front of hundreds of people to give a speech, but now it comes so naturally. I'd even go so far as to say I enjoy it; after all, by talking about my cancer and the daily struggles it brings, perhaps I can make someone else's experiences with their illness more positive, or even save a life one day. I try and use social media as much as possible, and frequently post to the charity's Facebook page to encourage young women to check their breasts. I know better than some how breast cancer can affect young women who may never have considered it a possibility. One day I received an email to say that, because of my most recent post, a lady had checked herself and found a lump. Luckily it turned out to be nothing, but she confessed that without my post she might never have discovered it. Stories like this really do make everything worthwhile.

As well as running The Wedding Wishing Well Foundation I also do a fair amount of work for Breast Cancer Care and a charity called Bosom Buddies, which offers funding for 'buddies' – ladies who have had breast cancer who then go into schools to talk to young women about the disease. I am so passionate about raising awareness of breast cancer, and believe that these young people should be able to recognise signs of the disease and seek treatment as soon as possible. The ultimate dream would be to ensure that most cancers could be found in time to treat them effectively, as so often timing is a huge factor in whether someone survives or not. I was truly honoured to be asked to speak at The Karen Trust Lily Ball. The charity had helped to fund our wedding, so I was thrilled to be able to speak and encourage people to donate to their cause. I was presented with a bunch of flowers afterwards, and even got to meet Ian Wright! The perks of the job, eh?!

In April we helped a lovely couple from Birmingham who wanted to marry in East Sussex. The groom had advanced testicular cancer, and when I met them, Peter was so sick he was sleeping in a put-up bed in their front room. I could see the pain in his eyes and hoped that giving him a wedding to focus on would help him through the treatment that lay ahead. The bride, Charlotte, was studying to be a midwife, while Peter had been reading law at university. They should have been leading carefree lives, planning their future together with many years ahead of them. Instead they were dealing with this reality at such a young age; it was heartbreaking. Peter and his family were particularly keen on steam trains, so the wedding needed to have a vintage theme throughout.

We had even arranged for them to have some photos with a steam train at the local train station afterwards. As always, I shed several tears during the vows, and then hurried away to busy myself so that I didn't blub too loudly. Once again, it was a huge honour to be able to help such a lovely couple, although I always wished that it could be under different circumstances.

It was around this time that Johnsons Dry Cleaners, a fantastic corporate supporter of the charity, launched a Wedding Dress Amnesty in our honour. Each branch of the cleaners accepted donations of wedding dresses, suits, bridesmaids' outfits, fancy frocks and outfits, shoes, jewellery and accessories, which could then be cleaned and passed on to the charity. The volunteers and I would then be able to pass items on to our couples, or sell them to raise further funds for the charity – it was a brilliant idea, ensuring that members of the public from across the country had somewhere to take their precious wedding garments. The amnesty was originally supposed to span the month of June, but is still going strong today; it really heartens me to know that so many brides are happy to part with their treasured dresses so that another couple may be able to experience the joy of a wedding day.

As part of the amnesty I was invited onto Sky News to talk about it. Walking into that huge building in London was such a surreal experience – my first turn as a television star! The presenters, Stephen Dixon and Gillian Joseph, were lovely and really put me at ease. There was no time for me to be nervous, as I was dragged out of hair and make-up and onto the set before the artists had even had the chance to begin working. While the studio was full of cameras, none of them were manned, and so it was easy to forget they were even there. It felt a little like chatting to friends on the sofa in my living room. Following the recording of my piece, Devon was invited on set and everyone made a huge fuss of him, even letting him take a spin in the presenters' chairs.

Later that year, during the summer, I received the upsetting news that Emma, the charity's very first bride, had passed away. I was incredibly proud that we'd been able to give her and Steve just over eight months of married life together; I knew that it had meant so much to the couple and their families.

The weddings and hundreds of applications kept coming. There were many wonderful opportunities coming my way too, including trips to my local radio station Tone FM, and I always try to do as much as possible. This often spreads me very thin and I'm always conscious that sometimes Graham and Devon may feel neglected. I try and take them with me as much as I can so that they can experience these wonderful things with me. I see every occasion as a new memory for Devon to hold onto when I'm no longer around, and am so grateful that we get to experience so much together.

In October 2013 I was selected to be one of the models for the Breast Cancer Care Annual Fashion Show. The audience comprised family and friends, sponsors, and celebrities such as Denise Lewis, Gloria Hunniford, Nina Wadia, Cherie Blair and Edith Bowman. I was one of 22 men and women who made their way down the catwalk that day, each of us having been diagnosed with breast cancer during our lives. We all had body hang-ups too, whether it was increased weight caused by medication, or the scars that had been accumulated during numerous surgeries. When we met, though, we all had cancer in common and bonded straight away.

Sadly, one of the models, Sally, passed away before the Fashion Show, and another, Claire, has since died. Having cancer, and being a part of this world, means that death becomes part of the process; it's all around. One thing I have noticed about those of us diagnosed with these diseases is that we all live life to the full, as if our illnesses have given us a new lease of life. I have realised how lucky I am to wake up each morning and enjoy a blue sky, or hear a dawn chorus. Walking out in front of all those people during the Fashion Show was liberating, as well as emotional, and I now have a tight group of friends whom I could call upon to cry, or rant, with. We will be friends for ever.

I have been extraordinarily lucky in that all of my friends have always been very supportive. I have a small group of very close female friends who I would trust with my life. We spend as much time together as possible, as none of us knows when it might be the last time, and we are always careful to say 'I love you' to one other. Sometimes those three words aren't said enough. I know that one day my cancer will spread and it will affect my mobility even further, or mean that I cannot get out to do so many of the things that I enjoy now. I take each day as it comes, making the most of every moment.

Towards the end of 2013 I had a surprise phone call from someone at the *Daily Mail*. I was in for a shock; I was informed that Breast Cancer Care had nominated me for the paper's annual Inspirational Woman of the Year Award. It was wonderful to have been nominated by such an incredible charity and I was chuffed to bits that my name had come to mind. The paper's representative told me that I was one of the award's finalists, and that I had been invited to London for the ceremony, as well as an afternoon tea with Samantha Cameron at Downing Street. I was gobsmacked and must have looked like a goldfish! Going to Number 10 was one of the many things on my 'bucket list', and here I was about to tick it off! Graham, my parents, and representatives from Breast Cancer Care and Johnsons Dry Cleaners were all going to be filmed talking about me and The Wedding Wishing Well Foundation, and the video was to be used by the judging panel to help them make their decision.

Graham and I were given an expenses-paid trip to London, travelling up by train – a special treat in itself! We arrived at a gorgeous hotel in central London and were due to meet the other finalists and representatives from the *Daily Mail* in its conference room for lunch, before getting changed into outfits that had been donated by Jacques Vert especially for the occasion. It was lovely, and very humbling, to meet the other finalists; each one of them had the most extraordinary tale to tell.

As we drove towards Downing Street we all looked at each other with excitement. We were soon at the famous gates, and jumped out to be met by security. Soon we were standing at the big black door. It was the most surreal moment of my life. The door opened and we were all shown into one of the many rooms at the back of the building, where Samantha Cameron was waiting for us. She is absolutely beautiful in real life, and even taller than she appears in the media. She showed such a genuine interest in what we had to say. Another surprise then walked into the room – it was Bruce Forsyth, who was also utterly charming. The finalists and I had several photos taken with both Mrs Cameron and Bruce, as a photo of the winner would be used in the newspaper the following day. After the photoshoot we were all given a little tour around the building, which was fascinating. One of the PAs there said what a shame it was that Graham and Devon hadn't been able to come along too, and I explained how gutted my husband had been. She handed over her business card and insisted that I contact her to arrange another visit, this time with my boys in tow, when the famous Christmas tree was up. Graham was thrilled to hear about the visit to Downing Street, and I promised him we'd organise it soon.

As soon as we were ready we headed down the hotel's function room for the awards ceremony. Everywhere I turned there were famous faces that I recognised from the television, including Michael Buerk, Christopher Biggins, Bruce Forsyth again, Sian Williams, and even the members of Bananarama; I was in star-spotter's heaven! As we sat and watched, each of the finalists' videos was shown in turn. I saw each person's story come to life upon the big screen and it dawned on me just how hard the judging process must have been; it was far too difficult for me to pick a winner, everyone seemed so deserving. Following each video, we were called onto the stage to receive our finalist's award. Mine was presented just after I'd watched a clip of my dad talking about his pride for me, so, as usual, I was in tears by the time I reached the stage.

The final video had been shown, and the last finalist's award given; this was it. There was a big drum roll and I heard the words, 'and the winner is …' The room was so silent, and you could literally feel the anticipation. What followed was a pause that seemed to last a lifetime, although it must have been only a few seconds.

'… Naomi Thomas!'

Had they really just said my name? They couldn't have! My head was in my hands as the reality dawned. It really was me. I had won!

Chapter Nineteen

The prize for winning the *Daily Mail*'s Inspirational Woman of the Year award was £5,000 to spend on a holiday. It was just what we needed as a family, and I was really looking forward to taking time out to spend with my boys. We decided to divide the money into two holidays: one week in Goa, India, and a two-week break to Egypt, where we'd been for our honeymoon. My parents and I have been going to Goa for years and we have family friends who live there. I couldn't wait to take my husband and son to meet them for the first time. It would also be my dad's 65th birthday while we were there; it had been five years since my last trip, before my diagnosis.

In January the charity put together its best wedding so far; I was so proud to have been a part of that amazing day. As well as terminally ill people we also help those with life-limiting illnesses, and one application had caught my eye. It was from a couple in Essex who had three children. The groom had

Huntingdon's Disease, and it was heartbreaking to read about the difficult few years that they'd had. I read up on the disease after getting their letter and realised just how horrible the prognosis is for sufferers. While their life expectancy is much longer than that of many of our applicants, their quality of life deteriorates very rapidly. It was just as important for this couple to get married as it was for someone who had less time; for the groom to be able to walk down the aisle unaided was as good a reason as any as far as I was concerned.

I went to meet the couple in Essex and it felt so good to be able to tell them that we could help. We worked for several months to put together their dream wedding day. It meant three days away from home and my boys, but I knew that it would be worth it. As I stood at the back of the room, watching the bride, Emma, walk down the aisle, I was yet again in tears. The couple looked so in love and, as childhood sweethearts, I knew just how much it meant to them to be standing there taking their vows. Jason, the groom, was bowled over by his bride and shone with pride throughout the day. We had achieved a truly spectacular day for the couple, from the confetti and dress, to a children's entertainer, and gorgeous bouquet. The charity's volunteers and I pride ourselves in being able to put on fairytale weddings for our couples. Despite the change in circumstance we found that suppliers were just as willing to donate their time and services.

We recently organised our second wedding for a couple affected by Huntingdon's Disease. Again, they were such a deserving couple, and I was desperate for the wedding to be truly amazing for them. We pulled it off with great aplomb, and I sincerely hope that we can keep upping the game as far as our weddings are concerned.

In February it was once again time for us to celebrate the dedication of our volunteers, as well as the achievements of local wedding suppliers. The Bristol and Somerset Wedding Awards was the first ever awards ceremony to celebrate the talents of suppliers in my locality, and we combined the event with The Wedding Wishing Well Foundation Appreciation Awards to create something truly spectacular, perhaps even our best to date. I was blown away by the elegance of the venue, the dedication of the volunteers and the sheer generosity of those in attendance; on the night itself we raised over £1,200 for the Foundation. I was also immensely proud to see the turn-out. The Wedding Wishing Well Foundation was barely two years old and yet we were touching so many people.

That night we handed out several awards to our own volunteers, as well as a host of trophies in just about every category you can think of. The awards were such a success that 2015's ceremony is also on the cards; watch this space!

And so to the present day.

My latest MRI scan revealed that my cancer remains stable, although I know that this won't always be the case. One day it will spread, and when that happens it will be very difficult to say how long I have left. I make sure that every day counts, putting everything that I have into my family and The Wedding Wishing Well Foundation – I need to know that I have left lasting happy memories for my son; a way for him to remember me when I am gone. It also reassures me to know that I have done everything I can to help brides and grooms in my situation. Marrying my soul mate has meant everything to me – why shouldn't everyone else be afforded that right?

We've just got back from our fantastic trip to Goa. I left my laptop and phone at home and had a week of total relaxation; it was bliss, for all of us! Seeing our friends who live in Goa, leading totally different lives from our own, put everything into perspective and reminded me just how lucky I am. I may not have my health but I have so many other things: a healthy child, a fantastic and supportive husband, and a network of family and friends upon whom I can always rely. I have a roof over my head, and a charity that I absolutely live for. I have had some truly incredible experience and opportunities; I count my blessings every day.

I never thought that I would ever release my own book, but hope that it can help those who are going through cancer too. I want them to know that the disease doesn't have to rule or ruin their lives; in fact, it can be embraced, and give you a whole new lease of life. It may seem to everyone that I never stop and am always on the go, but there are days that only Graham sees when I'm confined to my bed. I really believe that coming to terms with my prognosis has helped massively. I can't change anything, so why waste time worrying about it?

Perhaps a miracle will occur and a new drug will be manufactured that has the ability to save me, and those like me around the world. The reality is that this probably won't be in my lifetime, but I don't worry about myself. My thoughts are always on Graham, Devon, and my family and friends; those who will be left to pick up the pieces and come to terms with it all. However, I always want them to remember that, despite the hardships and nightmares along the way, these have been the best years of my life. After all, how many people my age can say they have lived their lives to the fullest? I know that Graham will have the full support of our family and friends, and that Devon will never want for anything. He may grow up without a mummy, but Graham is a fantastic dad and will slot into his new 'mummy' role just as well.

Maybe one day Graham will even remarry; he has my full blessing. I will always be Devon's mummy, though, and no one can ever take that away from me. Having my son, particularly under the circumstances, was the biggest and best achievement of my life, and I hope that he will be able to look back upon my achievements and be proud of me. I also hope that the charity will keep going from strength to strength, continuing as my legacy.

I see my cancer as an inconvenience to my life, nothing more or less. It doesn't define me, or change who I am, although it has certainly altered my life unimaginably. I am eternally grateful for the opportunities and experiences I have been afforded since my diagnosis, and cannot imagine my life without the amazing people I have met in the last few years. Despite life's uncertainties, I look forward to every new adventure that still lies ahead with bated breath.

I say, 'Bring it on, cancer – I'm not done yet!'

Dedications and Thank Yous

Graham What a roller-coaster it's been. Through everything you've always been there for me. This was never part of the plan when we got together, but we've made the most of a bad thing. You and I were made to be together; you're my best friend and, although all of this may not be for as long as we had hoped, you'll always be the love of my life and be forever engraved on my heart.

Devon You are my little miracle, and all of this is for you. I hope you are one day proud of all that I have achieved. I love you to the moon and back again, 'in a rocket ship'!

Cancer You may not have been welcome but you have changed my life, strangely for the better. As much as I want you to 'do one' I owe you a lot too.

Aunty Sue For your support always!

My mum and dad We've had our ups and downs, but I really do love you.

Sam Williams We owe you so much. Thank you from the bottom of our hearts.

Mary Poppins, The Karen Trust and the suppliers at our wedding You made our wedding happen. Thank you for completing our hearts.

Dream-A-Way For an amazing honeymoon full of special memories.

The *Sidmouth Herald* Without your coverage our wedding and the charity would never have got underway.

My close friends, Shari, Hev, Pen, Paula, Lucy, Tanya, Kiri and Katie You are all always there for me. You each bring something different to my life. I love you all so, so much.

Mary Gill, Jo Robbins and Lee Bishop You are all key to the charity, but most of all you have become amazing friends of mine who I trust with my life.

Louise Baker For helping me to write the book. I simply couldn't have done it without you.

HarperCollins Thank you for giving me this amazing opportunity.

Johnsons Dry Cleaners You've supported us with such a great idea, and you never ask for anything in return. Thank you for raising our profile and for believing in the charity, and me. You really are help-ing to change lives.

Breast Cancer Care, James Campbell and the *Daily Mail* So much has come from my award, and the memories we've made through the holiday prize will last with us for ever.

Dr Khan and Linda at Kingsmill Hospital, Nottinghamshire You helped us through a dark time, and helped us to make decisions that mean I am still here.

Trisha and all my nurses at Health Care at Home You always bring joy to my three-weekly treatments. Thank you for literally helping to keep me alive.

Dr Barlow at Musgrove Park Hospital, Taunton Thank you for always giving me time.

My English teacher and tutor, Mr Long Look, I wrote a book!

All my volunteers and suppliers You are key to the past and future of the charity. I may often get the majority of the glory, but the truth is I, and the charity, are nothing without you.

Our brides and grooms past, present and future Thank you for continuing to inspire me.

To all of those I've forgotten Sorry! These days my brain is like a sieve. You know who you are and what you mean to me!

Moving Memoirs

Stories of hope, courage and the power of love…

If you loved this book, then you will love our
Moving Memoirs eNewsletter

Sign up to...

- Be the first to hear about new books

- Get sneak previews from your favourite authors

- Read exclusive interviews

- Be entered into our monthly prize draw to win one
  of our latest releases before it's even hit the shops!

Sign up at

www.moving-memoirs.com